"Jeff Baxter has done a masterful job of communicating the powerful truth of teens and adults working together to transform the body of Christ."

Dr. David Olshine
Chair of Youth Ministries, Columbia International University

"Congregations must become inclusive communities on the life journey together rather than loosely connected groups divided by generation and life situation. *Together* provides a road map for that journey."

Diane R. Garland, PhD
Author of *Family Ministry*

"A growing number of youth workers have been talking about the importance of intergenerational ministry, but Jeff Baxter, thankfully, causes us to take a step back (so we understand the *why* of intergenerational ministry) and takes us several steps forward (with suggestions for *how*)."

Mark Oestreicher
Author of *Youth Ministry 3.0*

"Jeff Baxter persuasively presents a new way of thinking about youth ministry and then provides a clear plan for churches to implement this needed vision. I highly recommend this book for pastors, youth workers, and all those who care about the next generation."

Dr. Bill Jones
President, Columbia International University

"As a father of four children, I resonate with Jeff Baxter's emphasis on intergenerational ministry. I believe the web of relationships adolescents create will be missing critical threads without important role models."

Steve Moore
President and CEO, The Mission Exchange

"Within these pages, Baxter hits on several core topics you'll need to know and apply in order to help lead the emerging generation into a fully alive relationship with Jesus Christ. Don't settle for anything less!"

Tony Myles
Lead Pastor, Connection Church

"The witness of the church and the future of our children will depend on whether we adults are willing to stand *Together* and love on the coming generations. This has to be the future of youth ministry!"

Dr. Steven Bonner
Professor of Youth Ministry, Lubbock Christian University

"Jeff has written a well-documented, easily readable book that addresses not only how to understand the millennial generation, but also how to effectively disciple them."

Dr. Kyle R. Greenwood
Assistant Professor of Old Testament, Colorado Christian University

"*Together* is a realistic picture of how the family can equip a generation of teens to respond to God's call on their lives. Jeff's emphasis on mind-set over model is refreshing, sustainable, and most of all, in line with God's plan for the family."

Chris Norman
Lead Pastor, Grace Gathering

"Dr. Baxter is presenting critical truths with practical answers, which could dramatically enhance long-term discipleship, slow the rapid turnover of youth pastors, and salvage a multitude of young adults who wander aimlessly away from the church when the youth party is over."

Dr. Dwight Robertson
Author of *You Are God's Plan A ... and There Is No Plan B*

"Jeff's well-researched and understandable book is thought provoking and reflective while at the same time very practical. A must read for every youth worker, parent, professor, and pastor!"

Dr. Kevin Turner
Professor of Youth Ministry, Colorado Christian University

"The message of *Together* is vital for the church."

Dr. Tim Elmore
Author of *Generation iY*

"Dr. Baxter offers a clear and convincing call for intergenerational ministry, providing stong examples for how this plays out in spritual growth that sticks around for the long haul."

Will Penner
Resource Director, The Center for Youth Ministry Training

"How do adolescents fit in the church? *Together* defines and rebuilds a solid youth ministry ecclesiology. Every pastor, youth professional, and parent must read this book."

Dr. Larry Lindquist
Assistant Professor of Pastoral Ministry and Evangelism, Denver Seminary

"*Together* calls church leaders back to the heart of God's plan for reaching and releasing the next generation—the families they grew up in and the whole church they attend."

Dan Luebcke
Pastor of Student Ministries, Southern Gables Church

"This is a must read for all who desire to see the church of Jesus Christ flourish today in our postmodern world."

Dr. Stephen R. Lewis
President, Rocky Mountain Bible College and Seminary

"Deeply grounded in sociological and biblical reflection coupled with a pastor's heart for discipleship and evangelism, *Together* offers us a clear picture of ministry for the twenty-first century."

Dr. Jeffrey F. Keuss
Author of *Freedom of the Self*

Jeff Baxter

Foreword by Mark DeVries

TOGETHER

ADULTS AND
TEENAGERS
TRANSFORMING
THE CHURCH

 youth
specialties

ZONDERVAN.com/
AUTHORTRACKER
follow your favorite authors

ZONDERVAN

Together
Copyright © 2010 by Jeff Baxter

YS Youth Specialties is a trademark of YOUTHWORKS!, INCORPORATED and is registered with the United States Patent and Trademark Office.

This title is also available as a Zondervan ebook. Visit www.zondervan.com/ebooks.

Requests for information should be addressed to:

Zondervan, *Grand Rapids, Michigan 49530*

Library of Congress Cataloging-in-Publication Data

Baxter, Jeff.
      Together : adults and teenagers transforming the church / Jeff Baxter.
        p.   cm.
      Includes bibliographical references (p.   ).
      ISBN 978-0-310-57874-1
      1. Church work with teenagers. 2. Teenagers and adults—Religious aspects—Christianity. I. Title.
    BV4447.B39 2010
    259'.23—dc22   2010037313

Cover design: SharpSeven Design
Interior design: David Conn

Printed in the United States of America

10 11 12 13 14 15 16 17 18 /DCI/ 24 23 22 21 20 19 18 17 16 15 14 13 12 11 10 9 8 7 6 5 4 3 2 1

To all those who dare to dream about the future of faithful youth ministry that dances together with all generations.

CONTENTS

Appendixes

FOREWORD

THE POWER OF VERTICALITY

Mark DeVries

For almost two decades now, the world of youth ministry has been on a clear trajectory. Across theological, denominational, and geographical lines, more and more of us have embraced the unparalleled power of partnering with parents and connecting our teenagers to an intentional constellation of godly adults in our churches.

But the sad fact remains that most "successful" youth ministries continue to choose the path of least resistance, isolating teenagers into comfortable, horizontal ghettoes of well-wired youth rooms. Despite our infatuation with technology, facilities, and our own creativity, most churches do youth ministry in a way that virtually guarantees spiritual immaturity.

This is an environment for ministry that rewards youth leaders more for coolness than Christlikeness, that downgrades the definition of "Christian community" to church-connected teenagers socialized into talking, dressing, and even standing like one another.

I call it the trap of *horizontalization*. (Yes, I did make up that word.)

Horizontalization is the practice of isolating youth into structures that (often unintentionally) limit their interactions in the church to those most like them. Though horizontalized youth ministries may spend millions on facilities and technologies, those investments, in many contexts, only exacerbate the fundamental problem—the generational isolation of youth.

Horizontalization is easy. Horizontalization is always more comfortable than the *Together* alternative. Given the choice, youth (okay, maybe the rest of us, too) will choose to remain in the comfort and protection of their own peer clusters. But the sad reality is that when Christian teenagers spend most of their time with their peers, there is minimal chance of them learning much beyond what their friends know (which is, by and large, what they already know themselves).

We're learning the hard way that, in the long run, horizontalized youth ministry is simply not a very effective context for growing lifelong disciples of Jesus Christ.

Ultimately, verticality wins the day.

While horizontalized youth ministries might be more comfortable, they have the potential to keep our ministries sterile and stale (despite our desperate attempts at "outrageous," "cutting-edge," and "explosive" programming). Vertical youth ministries, on the other hand, have the power to create freshness and momentum by introducing the unpredictable, catalytic ingredient of strangers from other generations.

We saw that power firsthand just a few months ago in our congregation.

VERTICALITY EXPERIENCED

For a decade or so, our church had a tradition of *grade-level* mission trips. Those entering ninth grade would go one place, the sophomores would go another, all the way up to the graduating seniors—five different mission trips every summer. This past year, driven partly by a need to protect the sanity of our youth staff), we announced that we'd be putting all our 9th–12th graders together on a single trip to New Orleans.

I thought I would have a mutiny on my hands.

Our youth, parents, and leaders "trusted us," but they were wary and unconvinced. The pull of the horizontalizing—the "my class," "my kids," "our grade's trip" mentality—was mighty strong . . . until the group experienced the power of verticality at its best.

Before the 9th–11th graders arrived, our 12th graders spent a day training to lead their teams and to "welcome the stranger" in the form of younger students they did not yet know. And by the end of the trip, it was unanimous:

No more grade-specific trips.

The momentum created by simple verticality—giving seniors leadership and intentionally mixing the grades—was somehow different, more anchored than on our one-grade-level-only trips. The adults were available, not to stay busy running the work sites, but to support the seniors in their leadership and to be free to build multigenerational connections with all the students.

Like the difference between a stake driven into the ground and a stake lying on the ground, the vertical approach is more stable, more elevated, and less vulnerable to the winds of changing culture. There's no doubt it is much easier just to lay the stake on the ground; but unless the stake is driven into the vertical position, it simply cannot accomplish what it's been created to do.

SO WHY ANOTHER BOOK?

Despite the growing passion for "family-based youth ministry," translating that passion into action has been, and continues to be, well, hard.

It's hard enough simply getting *kids* to show up at our youth programs, much less trying to get their parents involved. It's hard enough getting our *youth* to start conversations with one another, much less trying to get adults and youth to talk together. And some churches have made it a structural and scheduling impossibility for the generations to even cross paths—with "big church" worship occurring acres and hours away from youth gatherings. All in all, bringing the generations together can feel, at times, downright impossible.

Jeff Baxter and I, along with hundreds of other leaders in youth ministry today, remain fiercely committed to a vision of empowering parents and connecting youth to rich constellations of relationships with godly adults. And though Jeff and I may come from different branches of the church family tree (a clear evidence that the Holy Spirit just might be at work), we share the same heartbeat when it comes to seeing family-based youth ministry become viral throughout the church.

I shudder to think where my own children would be if it hadn't been for their church family (not just their youth group!). They're all grown now, but when I think about the impact the great cloud of witnesses at our church had on their lives, I want to spend every ounce of energy I have left paying our church back and helping other churches do the same for their kids.

Our youth ministries must become more than yet one more horizontalizing context for our youth. And we youth pastors must seize every opportunity to verticalize our ministries.

May *Together* help us take the next few steps forward along the journey of recalibrating our investment in the next generation, so that we may more faithfully equip young people to live as lifelong disciples of Jesus Christ.

Mark DeVries is the author of Family-Based Youth Ministry *and* Sustainable Youth Ministry. *He is also the founder of Youth Ministry Architects (www.ymarchitects.com), a youth ministry consulting team that helps churches build sustainable, deep-impact youth ministries. Since 1986, Mark has also served as the associate pastor for youth and their families at First Presbyterian Church in Nashville, Tennessee.*

ACKNOWLEDGMENTS

A few years ago, I never would have imagined I'd be writing a book about connecting the generations together in faithful ministry. But as I have read books and researched the subject; watched the changes in adolescents over the years; spoken with youth workers across the country; worked in the trenches of the local church in many contexts; meditated on the Scriptures; read plenty of "blog feedback"; and continued to seek to live as close as possible to the Father, Son, and Holy Spirit, I have fallen in love with a very old idea: We simply need to find as many ways as we can for different generations to connect and share with one another their stories of faith in God.

I am thankful to so many people for this opportunity. In my first book, *Following Jesus into College and Beyond*, I tried to think of as many different creative ways to say thank you to all the people who'd helped me along the way. This time, I simply want to express my thanks to the Triune God for his grace and guidance; to my wife, Laurie, and my kids, Lillian, Levi, and Lara for their love; to the many people whose wise thoughts on "intergenerational ministry" issues have shaped this book, to the publishing team at Zondervan and Youth Specialties (especially Jay Howver for believing in this idea and Doug Davidson for challenging my thinking and making this book better); to Mark DeVries for raising awareness nearly 20 years ago and writing the foreword to this book; and to Foothills Bible Church for giving me the opportunity to live this stuff out in a real ministry context. Thanks to all of you!

Finally, I want to thank *you*—the reader—for being interested in what I have to say and for your willingness to take risks in putting these principles into practice. I am so very grateful to be part of this conversation with you.

May God be glorified as we work together to transform the church.

INTRODUCTION: INTERGENER . . . WHAT?

MOVING TOWARD A NEW MINDSET FOR YOUTH MINISTRY

inter- (prefix) from Latin, meaning "between," "among," "in the midst of," "mutually," "together"

generation (noun) 1. the entire body of individuals born and living at about the same time: *the postwar generation*. 2. A group of individuals, most of whom are the same approximate age, having similar ideas, problems, attitudes, etc.

together (adverb) 1. indicating that people are with one another, or that something is done with another person or other people, or by joint effort. 2. in company with others in a group or in a place. 3. interacting, communicating, or in a relationship with one another. 4. cooperating with one another or by joint or combined effort.

—http://encarta.msn.com

GOOGLE IT!

If you turn on your computer and search for the word *ministry,* you come up with a monstrous 184 million hits on this word. If you search for the word *intergenerational,* you would land on nearly 2.5 million hits. A search for the phrase *intergenerational ministry* generates nearly 1 million hits. When I set out to write a book about an intergenerational approach to ministry—and particularly youth ministry—I was surprised by the amount of attention the topic was receiving. This is a big topic that's being discussed not only on the Internet, but also in academic classrooms, research institutions, and churches and youth ministries across the globe. Many, many people are talking about it.

But what is "it"?

To put it simply, "intergenerational ministry" is bringing together people of different generations so they all might grow in godliness. This can be accomplished in many different ways in the local church and other ministry contexts, but I am convinced that an intergenerational approach to ministry can transform the church. The older generations have "God stories" to offer the younger. Our youth have a fresh enthusiasm and passion for God that can breathe new life into the adults. Yet too often our churches and ministries isolate the generations—and fail to recognize the importance of bringing adults and teenagers together.

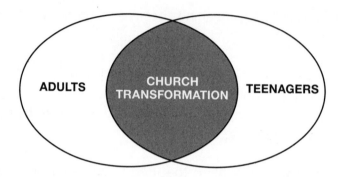

Throughout Scripture, we find stories and teaching about the importance of connecting across generational lines. The Psalmist declares, "Even when I am old and gray, do not forsake me, my God, till I declare your power to the next generation, your mighty acts to all who are to come" (Psalm 71:18). Or consider the advice Paul shares with his younger partner in ministry, Timothy: "And the things you have heard me say in the presence of many witnesses entrust to reliable people who will also be qualified to teach others" (2 Timothy 2:2). This is the veteran disciple Paul handing the essentials of the faith to young Timothy, so that Timothy might pass the faith to others who would, in turn, pass it to others.

As a youth pastor, I'm very aware of the critical role our older generations can have in discipling young people. But I'm also aware that it is not a one-way street. In biblical times and today, God also chooses the youth to impact those who are much older. Josiah became king of Israel when he was just eight years old (EIGHT!), ruled for 31 years, and "did what was right in the eyes of the LORD" (2 Kings 22:1–2). In his mid-twenties, this young king renewed his commitment to help all God's people to live fully for the Lord (2 Kings 23:3). *What passion!*

What we are really talking about when we speak of intergenerational ministry is an approach to ministry that is rooted in the very heart and being of God. The Triune God whom Christians worship is a God whose very nature is expressed in *relationships*.

We worship God in three persons—the Father, Son, and Holy Spirit—and those three are intimately related. If the heart of the God we worship is highly relational, I believe this should be a guiding principle for our ministry in the local church. Jesus prayed at the end of his earthly ministry for unity among all believers, praying, "that all of them may be one, Father, just as you are in me and I am in you. May they also be in us so that the world may believe that you have sent me" (John 17:21). As the church moves forward in faithful ministry, it requires the generations to be connected together, just as the Father, Son, and Holy Spirit are united. This was Jesus' prayer, and it should be our focus.

Then Jesus came to them and said, "All authority in heaven and on earth has been given to me. Therefore go and make disciples of all nations, baptizing them in the name of the Father and of the Son and of the Holy Spirit, and teaching them to obey everything I have commanded you. And surely I am with you always, to the very end of the age."

—Jesus, Matthew 28:18–20

Tell me how it is that in this room there are three candles and but one light, and I will explain to you the mode of the divine existence.

—John Wesley

In short, adults and teenagers working together to grow in faith and transform the living church is a thoroughly biblical approach that begins with the God we meet in the Scriptures. Intergenerational ministry is not just a trendy strategy, a way of offering support for burned-out youth workers, or a way of including youth in the worship service on Sundays. It is an expression of the very nature of God and his heart for the future of not only youth ministry, but also the entire church.

NOT ALONE

All sorts of Christian denominations, churches, and ministries are making conscious efforts to incorporate a cross-generational approach to their work. The many Christian groups taking steps to connect the generations span the spectrum of Christianity, including groups such as the Church of the Nazarene, the Evangelical Covenant Church, the Roman Catholic Archdiocese of Boston, the United Methodist church, the Southern Baptist Church in Kansas, Assemblies of God, Evangelical Presbyterian churches, Congregational churches, Greek Orthodox churches, Evangelical Free churches, a number of different Baptist groups, and many others. Church-based universities and research institutions are also pursuing intergenerational ministry with an intense focus. Dr. Steve Vandegriff of Liberty University has written on the importance of the topic online.[1] The Youth Institute at Fuller Theological Seminary has done significant research and study of the topic.[2]

> Isn't 'intergenerational youth ministry' contradictory? Maybe we should stop calling it youth ministry.
>
> —Brian, Youth Worker

As you can see, intergenerational ministry is a huge topic that many church groups are thinking about. There's no way to cover it fully in a single book. So why even try? Let me offer seven reasons why I decided to write *Together*:

1. First, I long for my own life as well as the ministry I'm part of to be in alignment with the one true God of the Universe. I believe God's desire has always been to bring the generations together so that all can grow closer to him in community (no matter the size of your local church or ministry).
2. I have a pastor's heart for the church. Having served for several years in local churches, I have experienced both the ugly and the heavenly. I long for her to be beautiful and faithful to her calling, giving God the glory. Connecting the generations in intentional ministry will set up the church for this end.
3. I am convinced that separate-island ministry that seeks to work with youth and young adults apart from the larger church will not be "working" with faithfulness five to ten years from now—and it may not be working now. We'll talk more about the ineffectiveness of single-generation approaches to ministry throughout the book.
4. I believe parents are and always will be one of the foundations of any effective ministry to children, youth, and young adults. An intergenerational approach recognizes the importance of parents and even grandparents in helping the younger generations grow in relationship with the Triune God.
5. We're in the midst of a changing culture that makes intergenerational ministry all the more essential. We'll talk more about these changes throughout the book. But

at a time when adolescence is extending later into life, sound theology is slipping, and negative cultural influences are spreading, we need a new mindset (which is actually an old mindset) for reaching the next generation for Christ Jesus.

6. On a personal note, as my three children approach their own teenage years, I'm realizing more and more the importance of helping them connect in meaningful relationships with all sorts of Jesus-following adults. Of course, this begins with my wife, Laurie, and me; but I believe a supportive intergenerational community of fellow Christians offers my children (and any children) the greatest chance of living an abundant life in God.

7. Finally (but certainly not in conclusion!), I believe we need a multitude of voices from every angle speaking up about this desperately needed topic. So many churches are experimenting with a more cross-generational approach, yet still struggling to get their "ministry minds" around what it means and how it works. My goal is to give you a new way of thinking about ministry as you seek to share Christ faithfully with the next generation. I want to increase the volume of the dialogue that's occurring on, in, and around churches, coffee shops, kitchen tables, porches, back decks, water coolers, passionate pulpits, living rooms, ministry offices, and board rooms about this important ministry mindset for connecting adolescents with what matters most.

To sum it all up, my desire in writing this book is to help focus the lenses through which we view ministry . . .

THE LENSES

In my own experience as a youth worker on the front lines and in the trenches, as well as my conversations with many other youth workers—including those fresh out of training from colleges or seminaries, or veterans still trying to "figure it out"—here is what I have found: We're studying and talking about all the right things in the field of youth ministry. We read and discuss theology, adolescent development, evangelism, family dynamics, and other important topics, all with the passionate hope of putting together an effective plan for reaching and discipling the next generation. We understand more and more that we can't effectively build up the body of Christ if our youth are left out on the youth ministry island, separated from the larger church. But when it comes to an intergenerational approach, we have trouble bringing all the pieces together and difficulty organizing and actually implementing it all. Brian, a youth worker I spoke with recently, expressed the confusion many of us feel in figuring out intergenerational ministry, when he said, "I could give you a book on this topic, but in my head it is a massive jumbled mess." I do not think he's alone.

When youth workers hit the ground running in youth ministry, we're aware of all the different forces that shape the lives of the teenagers we work with. Yet the competing demands clutter our thinking, and the tyranny of the urgent dominates the day (or the week, which then turns into years). Our vision for ministry becomes blurry. We find it hard to focus.

There's so much information in our heads that many youth workers, pastors, parents, and other volunteers struggle to develop a clear ministry plan and philosophy that will focus their efforts on transforming the church family together. We have visions of something dancing in our heads, but we compartmentalize our thinking because we're not sure how it all fits together. The jumbled mess looks something like this picture where our lenses for ministry are not lined up. The vision is fuzzy and so is our thinking.

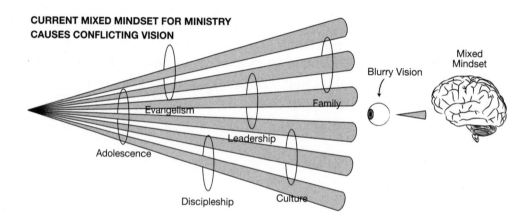

CURRENT MIXED MINDSET FOR MINISTRY CAUSES CONFLICTING VISION

Evangelism

Family

Leadership

Adolescence

Discipleship

Culture

Blurry Vision

Mixed Mindset

Throughout this book, I want to help youth workers focus their vision and clarify their thinking. I would like to help us develop a different ministry mindset where intergenerational connections are natural and central to ministry. The chapters that follow address each of these "lenses" through which we view youth ministry. All the lenses need to be lined up for effective ministry to take off. If they are a disorganized mess, if our vision is blurry and our thinking scattered, we will be ineffective in ministry or, worse, we will burn out and eventually quit our ministry post.

Take a look at the lenses in the picture below. With the lenses aligned, the vision becomes clear. As you read through the chapters addressing each of these lenses, keep in mind the big picture and where this focused energy is heading. The goal is to develop a new mindset for intergenerational ministry—a mindset that empowers teenagers and adults to do ministry together. As we line up these lenses, the light of the gospel shines through. The power of the Holy Spirit helps us focus so that we might be free to bear

fruit in the lives of the next generation and the church. It would look something like the next picture.

NEW FOCUSED MINDSET FOR INTERGENERATIONAL MINISTRY

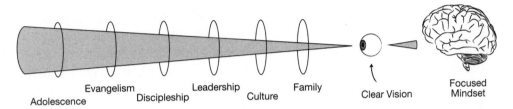

Adolescence   Evangelism   Discipleship   Leadership   Culture   Family   Clear Vision   Focused Mindset

ALIGNED LENSES FOR CLEAR VISION

THE GOOD NEWS AND BAD NEWS

Did you ever hear the story about the youth worker who was given a chance to write his own job description? (Which of us wouldn't like the opportunity to design our own job?) Well, the good news was that the church board accepted the job description exactly the way the youth worker wrote it. They didn't change a single word. The bad news was that the board was so inspired by the job description that they immediately formed a search committee to find somebody capable of doing the job! *Ouch!*

Throughout this book, as in much of life, there's both good news and bad news. We'll begin this book by taking a realistic look at the current state of the church's ministry to adolescents. Unfortunately, some of the findings are pretty discouraging. Families are moving at reckless speeds, often with little intentionality on helping kids become mature Jesus-following adults. There's more than a little bad news in these headlines. But ultimately, there's even more good news. There's the life-changing Good News of the gospel. And there's an incredible opportunity to transform our ministries in ways that will make a huge kingdom impact on not only our teenagers, but the entire church.

Then we'll spend a chapter on each of the individual "lenses." In chapter 2 we will get inside the heads of our teenagers by considering adolescent development. As you may know, the word *adolescence* is relatively new, and the changes that occur in this phase of development have significant ramifications for our ministries. In chapter 3 we will consider the spiritual significance of what is really happening in families today and how youth workers can partner with parents more effectively. Then in chapter 4 we'll take a look at youth culture—an area in which many youth workers are "experts."

This is good news, but adolescents are swimming upstream and sometimes get swept away by negative culture and influences. We need to turn the tide.

In chapter 5 we'll talk about the topic of leadership. My experience is that the word *leadership* is mentioned a lot among youth workers but not often deeply considered as a vital part of the future of ministry to youth. We'll take a look at youth ministry leadership, which is vital no matter what size church you serve. We'll focus on evangelism in chapter 6. All of us are in youth ministry to share the great news of Jesus Christ with teenagers and with the prayerful hope that they will embrace the salvation and abundant life that's available through the cross and the grace of God. In chapter 7 we'll look at the lens of discipleship and its significance and importance in ministry to youth. Maybe you prefer a different term like *mentoring* or *spiritual formation,* but I choose to use the word *discipleship* because of its connections to the first followers of Christ.

In the final chapter of this book, we will seek to realign all these lenses in a way that provides a clear vision for ministry. But let me make one thing clear: This book is intended to provide not a new *model* for ministry, but a new *mindset* for ministry. Many books have been written that suggest new and different models for how to reach and disciple youth—and some of them are quite valuable. I know. I think I have read most of those books and tried many of the models over the years. But constant change in models of youth ministry in the local church tends to exhaust youth workers—and frustrate senior pastors whenever a youth worker comes home from a conference and wants to flip the ministry upside down. Some youth conferences (and church leadership conferences) still seem to think there is only one particular model that is effective for ministry. The time of "one-size-fits-all" models is gone in youth ministry (and in adult ministry in the church).

We don't need more models. We need a new mindset that helps us think strategically about the whole church surrounding the next generation with love and care. We need to shift our thinking about the future faithfulness of ministering to youth. If we begin to refocus our thinking on how an intergenerational approach can help address the significant issues facing youth ministry today, we will be able to customize our ministry in our particular location and time in history. Our ministries won't all look the same or have the same "model," but each of us needs to bring together the same elements in a way that's best suited to our own situation. At the very end of the book, you'll find several appendixes that will help you talk about these ideas with the other leaders and parents in your own ministry context, evaluate how you are doing in ministry, and plan for the future.

Use the chapters to stir your thinking and dialogue with those around you about the critical topics that face faithful intergenerational ministry.

HOPE FOR A TIRED YOUTH WORKER

Dear Youth Worker,

Are you exhausted trying to keep up on the youth ministry treadmill and overwhelmed by the size of the task?

There is hope!

Father, Son, and Holy Spirit

HOPE FOR THE WEARY

I really believe the best days are ahead for reaching and discipling teenagers and their families in the body of Christ, but it's easy to get overwhelmed by the bad news. We have hard work ahead of us to turn the bad news into good for the glory of God.

Many youth workers are tired and discouraged, and some are even ready to give up. They started out with high hopes about reaching kids for Christ. But over time, the pressures built to the point of damage and depression. Youth workers are tired of the direction the local church is heading with its inflexible ministry practices (sometimes called "traditions"). They are weary of a world that seems to be taking away youth in the evil flood of culture. They are exhausted trying to keep up with the latest pop-culture fad or the bigger youth ministry down the block. They are disillusioned by thin theologies that dilute their practice of ministry. And they are discouraged by churches that have left them alone with the teenagers on their own "exile islands" of ministry. Some have even left the "institutional church" and created new forms of church (that really aren't new, but old partial forms of church). *what would that look like?*

(Doing youth ministry together) fully with all generations will alleviate some of the burden these youth workers are feeling. It takes multiple generations coming alongside teenagers to transform the church. It requires a team to carry the load.

If you are feeling discouraged, I urge you not to give up. Stay in the fight to reform and refocus the local church. We need all generations engaged for the future. I believe teenagers and young adults have potential to breathe new life into our churches. But I am afraid if we don't engage the next generation fully, the local church as we know it will die.

With open dialogue, honest strategic thinking, and hearts that are open to God's transforming power, we can help the next generation know Jesus and make him known. We can find peace and move forward in ministry. But without authentic dialogue and fresh thinking, we'll remain stuck in the same old mud—spinning our wheels aimlessly but getting nowhere.

Hidden away in the book of Ecclesiastes is this wise principle: "If the ax is dull and its edge unsharpened, more strength is needed, but skill will bring success" (10:10). We youth workers need to be intentional about staying sharp—first, through personal renewal with God and a community of Jesus-following believers called the church, but also with a youth ministry vision that is intentionally connected to the larger local church. This requires an honest diagnosis of the current state of youth ministry, a new mindset that dreams of what adults and teens might do in ministry together, and the passion to make this vision a reality.

"Do not lose heart," Paul urged the early Christians of the Corinthian church (2 Corinthians 4:1). I am sure he would say that same thing to youth workers today. We've been given a treasure in weak vessels, so that in our weakness Jesus Christ will be glorified more. If we were strong without Jesus, we would not need him or his power in our lives. Paul knew we needed to be made weak so we would need Jesus more. We might feel like a defenseless quarterback being rushed by an elder board full of 300-pound linebackers, but Paul says we will not be sacked (maybe fired, but not taken out of life with Jesus). We may feel stretched in every direction by our youth ministry schedule, but we will not snap with Jesus by our side. Like a deer in the woods, we might feel as though we're being hunted down by a huge pack of parents, but Jesus offers us the strength to keep going. We may even feel like we're in the boxing ring with a huge high school senior who'd love to knock us out, but the Scriptures promise that with Jesus at the center of our lives, we will not be overcome. Paul concludes 2 Corinthians 4 with the same thought with which he began: "Do not lose heart." This calling you have is worth every minute (2 Corinthians 4:1–16). Be hopeful!

Hang in there. The church needs you. The teens in your ministry need you. God wants to continue to use you to make him known. I believe we can bring healing to a hurting and sometimes damaging approach to local church youth ministry.

So grab a latté, pull up a chair, and let's start a fresh conversation. From the bottom of my heart, I thank you for joining me on this journey of connecting teenagers and adults so that all the generations might better know the transforming power of Jesus Christ.

1
WHAT'S REALLY HAPPENING?

THE YOUTH MINISTRY STATE OF AFFAIRS

Let the little children come to me, and do not hinder them, for the kingdom of God belongs to such as these.

—Jesus in Mark 10:14

What the whole church must face—local congregations and parachurch ministries alike—is the enormity of the need. The facts speak for themselves: Only 15 to 20 percent of American teenagers are significantly involved in a local church.

—Doug Burleigh, *Past President of Young Life*

Maybe you've heard it said that without proper diagnosis of an illness, the proper prescription for health is impossible. The same is true in ministry. Unless we're willing to acknowledge the problems with what we're doing currently, we'll never be able to dream of or implement ministries that are more faithful and effective. But diagnosing the problems requires transparency and honesty. Local church leadership, ministry point people, elders, senior pastors, parents, school administrators, coaches, and other caring adults need to be real. We need to be open and truthful. We need to disconnect our personal identities and our egos from our ministries and take an honest look at what we're doing. I know this is difficult, but let's ask for God's help and make the effort. Let's be honest with one another.

CALL 911   *is it?*

I believe youth ministry today is in critical condition. Our work with youth in most local churches is marred by a huge number of bruises, broken bones, and serious

25

lacerations. Many ministries are in the emergency room desperately in need of surgery. But why?

First, and most important, the reality is that many young people today couldn't care less about Jesus Christ and connecting to the body of Christ during their teenage years. Those teenagers who have been involved with a local church often leave it after completing high school. Few young people see the value in the local assembly of believers. They simply don't see any reason why church involvement is essential to their daily lives.[1]

I suppose I agree.

At the same time, the pressure and expectations placed on youth workers in many churches is misdirected and unfair. I have interacted with many youth workers who've been wounded on the front lines. They are exhausted from trying to keep up with the day-to-day demands of the job and never having the time and space to stop and think about the big picture.

Finally, there are outside forces placing incredible pressure on our ministries. The breakdown of the family, the negative influence of certain elements of youth culture, and the lengthening of adolescent development have all helped to put many youth ministries on life support.

The bottom line is this: The way we think and do youth ministry needs to change, or our efforts will never have the kind of impact we hope and pray for.

AMBULANCE EN ROUTE

Maybe you think I'm exaggerating. Things aren't really that bad. And I would not disagree that some congregations and ministries are discipling youth faithfully while connecting them to the local church. But overall we are tricking ourselves if we think youth ministry is operating at full faithfulness. I am not alone in my diagnosis.

We are losing youth to the world when they should be found within the local church. With good intentions, we have built separate programs for our teenagers, isolating them from the whole of the church and walling them off in their own programs and buildings, instead of helping them connect to a larger vision. Too many churches hire a youth "expert" (or two) and ask him or her to operate on an island. "Just don't disturb anything around here and reach lots of kids," is the vibe felt or even heard by those who are impacting the next generation.

Sure, these ministries have some "successes" with some teenagers coming to Christ and others being intentionally discipled as commissioned by Jesus. But overall we are doing a poor job of connecting youth to the larger church while they are still in their junior high, high school, and college years. I believe many youth workers know what's happening, but they do not have the passion or plan to change what they are doing. Specific statistics vary, but the overall trend is very clear: We are losing many students to the world before and after high school graduation—and failing to make connections with others who do not know Jesus as Savior.[2]

Your assessment is true to reality. I am finishing up a grad course on adolescent spiritual formation. I asked my students at the beginning if it were possible to develop/create adolescent disciples of Christ. Most argued for the affirmative. I asked them the same question at the end of the course after taking them through the environmental, cultural, psychosocial, and familial issues surrounding adolescent culture and development. Now, they are not so sure.

It is difficult to make adolescent disciples, but it is possible with God's help. We just need to be aware of the right areas. The early onset of adolescence along with the emergence of mid-adolescence is a reality most youth workers and churches are either not aware of or are not equipped to handle. Church leadership is either completely ignorant or does not want to face the truth—they are losing the right to present the truth! The issue then becomes: What next?

—Dr. Steven Bonner, Professor of Youth Ministry, Lubbock Christian University

I think most of us in youth work understand the importance of surrounding our teenagers with caring adults, partnering with parents, and connecting youth to the local church. But we fail to make it a priority. Urgent demands are calling to us from every direction. "Just show us the results" is heard from the front office. Every week has a new list of needs, with students in crisis, calls from concerned parents, expectations from other church leaders, lessons to prepare, retreats to plan, volunteers to train, and students who just need some hang-out time. Vision gets put on the back burner. There is no time to think about the differences between childhood, adolescence, and adulthood. There's no time to think strategically about connecting youth ministry programming to the church's overall vision. The youth ministry calendar isn't planned in conversation with the other ministries in the church. We fail to think about family needs, because we're told our job is to get lots of students in our youth programs. *Right?*

The average youth worker is struggling with his or her own financial future and has little time to think about the cost to the family with a junior high and high school student who want to go to all the events in the coming year. Most youth workers are up on the latest music, movies, pop-culture news, video-gaming options, clothing, and Academy Award winners; but they are totally disconnected from and disillusioned by their own church culture, ministry calendar, and leadership structure. We struggle to find the right mix of freedom in leading our ministries, while submitting to the leaders and vision of our churches. And some feel like the local church is actually a barrier to our effective ministry with kids because it feels "behind the times" and "irrelevant." I know youth workers who never even attend the churches that employ them. Some have created a "youth church" within the "larger church," not realizing they are limiting the next generation's involvement in the full body of Christ. *yes*

Youth ministry has for far too long operated as a rogue ministry separate from the rest of the life of the church. This is problematic in that, even the best youth worker in the most programmatic youth ministry gets limited time (and therefore influence) in the day-to-day life of a student compared to the time and influence that parents could have in the life of their teen. It does not model or teach for our teens biblical ecclesiology, which is why many high school graduates struggle with where they belong in the church after they move beyond youth group. The same thing can be said of college campus ministries that serve as an older youth group model that can perpetuate for a college student a certain idea of what it means to be a part of the church.

—Didi, Youth Pastor

Then there is the tension of needing more people to help with the youth program, but once people volunteer, many youth workers are hard pressed to train and manage the unique personalities, personal agendas, motivations, and desires of the team members. When everyone seems to be running in his or her own direction, it often seems easier just to do it "on your own." And even when we do get volunteers involved, rather than providing an essential connection to the whole of the church, those volunteers often end up operating out on "Youth Ministry Island" with us. In the midst of all this, there is no time to compare the youth ministry's mission statement with the mission statement of the overall church, or to have conversations and collaboration with the senior pastor and other church leaders about making youth an essential part of the church's larger ministry. The weekly demands are too great. Youth workers might even think it is a waste of time to stop and think strategically and intentionally about connecting youth to the overall mission of the local church. *It might if the church isnt ready for this!*

The first appendix at the end of this book (page 163) features the "*Together* Evaluation Tool," a survey designed to help you assess how your own ministry team is doing. Take a moment to fill out this evaluation before you go any further in the book. While the evaluation instrument isn't perfect, it will give you an opportunity to think about some of the key questions we'll be considering throughout the book so we can keep learning together.

PRESSURE BUILDING TO A BOIL

In his wonderfully insightful book called *Your First Two Years in Youth Ministry,*[3] Doug Fields includes a list of his top ten youth ministry commitments and provides scriptural support to back them. I think Doug's list offers some great advice; I wish I'd had it back when I started in youth ministry. Take some time to consider these Ten Commitments:

TEN YOUTH MINISTRY COMMITMENTS

1. I will move slowly. (Proverbs 14:15–16)
2. I will regularly check my motives and evaluate my heart. (Proverbs 20:8–12)
3. I will steer clear of the numbers game. (Matthew 18:12)
4. I will not criticize the past. (Philippians 3:13)
5. I will avoid the comparison trap. (Galatians 6:4)
6. I will focus on priorities. (Matthew 22:36–40)
7. I will pace myself. (Hebrews 10:36)
8. I will serve. (Matthew 20:26–28)
9. I will be a learner. (Proverbs 4:5, 13:20)
10. I will pursue contentment. (Philippians 4:11)

—Doug Fields

My guess is that most youth workers have a difficult time fulfilling all these commitments—and that's especially true for those who are new to the job. I don't think this struggle is because Doug's list is a bad one, nor is it because youth workers don't believe these commitments are important. I think we struggle because of the combination of students' apparent disinterest in deeper biblical understanding, leadership pressures from the church, and the seemingly overwhelming list of tasks we face each week. We lose track of these commitments because the storm is too great. Youth workers love to work with teenagers, but the expectations are often unclear, so we find ourselves running in circles. As a result, the average youth worker is worn down and weary because of the pressures inside and outside the local church to reach youth with the gospel, to train them up in maturity, and to connect them to the church body. This causes youth workers to lose their focus, their passion for youth ministry, and maybe even their jobs. Burnout sets in and frustration dominates the day.

Forgive me for painting a depressing picture of the current state of affairs in many youth ministries, but we need to be honest with one another and realistic about where we are. Maybe this description doesn't match your ministry setting. If that's the case, I am thrilled for you. Really. Praise the Lord for your ministry situation. But I'm afraid that what I've shared is an accurate portrait of the ministry realities facing many youth workers, parents, families, and churches.

Without a clear and true diagnosis, the prescription for health cannot be reached.

The local church is so "natural" at splitting us into age groups and offering programs to support this. We discourage the connection between people more than we admit, and even more so between age groups. Every activity that we do, every function we hold, every communication, should have an eye toward whether this is promoting intergenerational body life or further inhibiting it. The fact that we have to label this "intergenerational connections"—and we do need to—shows how far we've drifted from truly "normal" body life where the youngest is seamlessly connected to the oldest in relationship and where discipleship happens without the need for programs. We further need to redefine the role of parents back to how God describes the role—as the owners, the accountable ones for teaching their children spiritual matters. Parents need to be reintroduced to this and understand that we will give an account someday.

—Jim, Parent of Teenagers

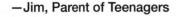

PRESSURE BUILDING FOR YOUNG PEOPLE

Of course, it's not just our ministries that are in crisis. The youth we work with are in a difficult spot themselves. More than 10 years ago, professor and author David Elkind wrote these words, "There is little or no place for adolescents in American society today—not in our homes, not in our schools, and not in society at large. We have, in effect, all but eliminated this age period as a distinct stage in the life cycle."[4] While we have had some good moments in youth ministry both inside and outside the church, overall things are getting worse for adolescents. Teenagers are often both labeled and treated as "grown-up children" or "little adults" by parents and other adults when they are neither. Many youth and young adults are never given a chance to "grow up" in a natural environment at a natural developmental pace. Society is forcing them to mature beyond their development. Unfortunately, Elkind's words are ever more true today.

Youth professional Kenda Creasy Dean affirms this idea when she writes, "The tension in youth ministry between protecting youth and empowering them still exists. The most promising models seem to be those that combine the protection of adolescents from premature adulthood with the empowerment of adolescents for ministry in their own right."[5] Most of us got involved with youth work because we wanted to walk alongside adolescents and help them grow up in Jesus, but the culture and developmental pressures on youth have changed and escalated in the last decade. It is a new and difficult day, which requires a new mindset for ministry.

It seems that we as a church have lost focus on the real matter here. Our youth are the future of our country, and we don't seem to be putting enough emphasis on them because they're not the ones paying our church bills. I understand that we need to keep a happy medium, but more focus needs to go toward them. There are some churches that are doing things the right way, and right now I am blessed to be a part of one of those churches. But I haven't always been, and those have left me very frustrated.

—Drew, Youth Ministry Volunteer

In research for my book, *Following Jesus into College and Beyond*, I sent out hundreds of questionnaires to high school and college-aged students across the nation. One of the questions asked young people what causes stress in their lives.[6] Their answers included the following: Making money, getting a job, finding housing, school, relationships, disappointing my parents, not sleeping, sports success, acceptance, picking the right friends, staying friends, sinning against God, trying to keep up with everything, wondering what will happen after high school, using time wisely, being bored, and "myself." The pressures adolescents face are growing. Ironically, while the average teenager might appear to be happy, relaxed, or even indifferent, under the surface many youth carry fear, loneliness, and hurt that few adults see or fully understand. Most adolescents believe their daily stress is as great as that of their parents. The causes of the stress might not be the same, but for the adolescent these troubles are very real. Today, adolescents live in what Dr. Chap Clark calls an "underground world," while the pressures and expectations of school, jobs, sports, and home life are forcing them into the adult world.[7] Pressure to become an adult quickly is pressing on our youth from every direction.

In *Passing on the Faith*, authors Merton Strommen and Richard Hardel tell us, "Americans are convinced that today's adolescents face a crisis—not in their economic or physical well-being but in their values and morals."[8] Furthermore, many families today are not orienting their teenagers toward lives of faith, service, and responsible living.[9] There are pockets of wonderful family connections across our communities and local churches. But is what most of us are doing in local church youth ministry right? Is operating on an island, separate from the "big adult church" and its vision and practice, really working? Are we really making mature Jesus-following adults? Or are we making good, safe, hardworking, and moral youth? There is a drastic difference.

Youth workers in partnership with the Triune God of the universe and the larger church family can bring healing to our ministry vision and wholeness to future generations if we adjust our thinking. A new mindset is needed. First, we need to take a closer look at the lenses of intergenerational ministry.

CLEARING KINKS FROM YOUR MINISTRY

There are few things as frustrating as when the water stops flowing while you are watering your grass or garden. Usually, it's not that the well has run dry, but that the hose you're using has developed a kink—it's bent in a way that prevents the water from flowing. So what do you do? You put down the end of the hose where the water is supposed to come out, walk back and undo the kink, and then walk back to where the water has now made a puddle. Yet before long—maybe even immediately—that same kink reappears, or a new one develops, and it stops the water again. So back and forth you go. Have you experienced this? You may even be tempted to go out and buy a new hose. Yet, in my experience, if I throw away the old hose and buy a new one, before too long the new one starts doing the same thing because I didn't take care of it like I should have.

Our ministries can develop kinks that stop them from flowing as they should. Sometimes we cause the kinks ourselves; other times it's just the circumstances of church or ministry life that cause the kink. Sometimes it's a lack of information, faulty understanding, or unfocused thinking. In the remaining chapters of this book, we'll explore areas where kinks may have interrupted the flow of your ministry in connecting the next generation to God and the local church. My goal is to help you, your ministry team, your volunteers, and the parents understand the barriers and develop a new mindset for ministry that will allow God's Spirit to flow throughout our ministries.

CONTINUE THE CONVERSATION

1. Do you think this chapter provides a fair diagnosis of current youth ministry?
2. What is your own assessment of youth ministry in the local church?
3. What is going well and what is lacking in most youth ministries today?
4. How are you thinking about these issues in your context for ministry?
5. What material from this chapter should you be discussing with volunteers, parents, or church leadership?

2
GETTING INTO THEIR HEADS

UNDERSTANDING ADOLESCENT DEVELOPMENT

The concept of childhood, so vital to the traditional American way of life, is threatened with extinction in the society we have created.

—David Elkind

Never forget that the children of over-committed, harassed, exhausted parents are sitting ducks for the con men of our time.

—James Dobson

Age is foolish and forgetful when it underestimates youth.

—Irish Proverb

Getting your brain around the human brain is difficult. And that's especially true when it comes to the adolescent brain!

Do you want to hear something truly amazing? Did you know that the cerebral cortex of the human brain contains roughly 15 to 33 *billion* neurons depending on gender and age, and each of these neurons links with up to 10,000 synaptic connections? Each cubic millimeter of cerebral cortex contains roughly 1 billion synapses! These neurons communicate with one another by means of long protoplasmic fibers called "axons," which carry trains of signal pulses called "action potentials" to other parts of the brain and distant parts of the body, targeting them to specific recipient cells.

This is the Triune God's handiwork on display.

ISN'T GOD AMAZING?

Special surgeons have the challenging task of operating on the human brain every day somewhere in the world. They have trained for years in the best schools to understand and study the brain. Neurologists mess with brains every day. And yet there is still so much these experts cannot fully understand about how it all works.

And while it is difficult to understand the brain's functions, understanding someone's thoughts is nearly impossible. Yet youth workers, like surgeons, are charged with the task of understanding the thinking of the young people they are trying to reach with the gospel and train to become disciples of Jesus Christ. I would suggest that understanding the thinking of the developing adolescents we're working with might be even more difficult than brain surgery!

I think I hear an "Amen, brother" in the background!

The brain is the organ of destiny. It holds within its humming mechanism secrets that will determine the future of the human race.

—Wilder Penfield, *The Second Career*

CONSTRUCTION ZONE

The adolescent brain should be marked off with bright orange signs that say UNDER DEVELOPMENTAL CONSTRUCTION. Like those construction workers who use large machines to repair potholes and build new roads, God is hard at work developing the brain of every teenager. Studies show that adolescent brain development continues not just through the teenage years but all the way until age 25. Intuitively, those of us who minister to the next generation know the youth we work with are not fully developed by the time they reach their eighteenth birthdays. Every youth worker has seen even the most mature teenage leader make foolish choices in situations where the better decision seems quite obvious.

Years ago when I was serving as a high school pastor, one of our most gifted students made a dumb decision. John (not his real name) was one of the most creative and innovative 17 year olds I'd ever met. During his junior year, he was being paid by churches to develop multimedia presentations. He would show up early and leave late serving with faithfulness at the soundboard and in the band. Other students looked to his leadership and followed him. I met with him weekly to disciple him in godly living. One day he came to me crushed. He told me he'd allowed his sexual relationship with a girl to progress much too far while they were in his parents' basement watching a movie. John could not put into words why it happened. I tried to express my disappointment with a spirit of grace, but I found it hard to understand how a guy at the top of our leadership team, a young man who seemed to have it all together, could have made such a mistake. Certainly, other students were stumbling through adolescence, but not our student leaders—*or so I thought.*

A few years later, I pursued my doctorate in youth and family ministry at Fuller Theological Seminary, with an emphasis in the areas of theology, adolescent development, and youth culture. The doors to the adolescent world were opened for me. I began to understand better that John and other young people were developing at their own pace—not just in terms of faith maturity, but also psychosocial maturity. The students I was working with were different from children, for sure, but they were different from adults, too. And while those differences were due to many outside influences, those teens were also shaped by their own natural development.

Issues of adolescent development cannot be "solved" by good theology. Of course, we know that every human being has a sinful nature that must be fully surrendered to God. But the dynamics of psychosocial development are a reality in every teenager. We cannot ignore them if we are going to be faithful in ministering to the next generation.

The following quote from the Mentor Foundation helps explain why John made that decision years ago: "During adolescence, the parts of the brain that are responsible for expressing emotions and for seeking gratification tend to mature sooner than the regions of the brain that control impulses and that oversee careful decision making. As one expert puts it, the teenage brain 'has a well-developed accelerator but only a partly developed brake.'"[1]

Doesn't that reflect your experience with teenagers? So many kids are "all go" on their feelings without "stopping to think" about their choices. This is not just the reflection of a faith that is still maturing. It also reflects physical brain development. The simple truth is that although the brains of adolescents mature at a remarkable rate, the teenagers and young adults we work with are not yet functioning at full efficiency. Furthermore, Dr. Jay Geidd of the National Institutes of Health suggests that brain development is deeply affected by the choices teenagers make during adolescence. Geidd says, "It's a time of enormous opportunity and of enormous risk." He continues, "If a teen is doing music or sports or academics, those are the cells and connections that will be hard-wired. If they're lying on the couch or playing video games or [watching] MTV, those are the cells and connections that are going [to] survive."[2]

In other words, the road is still under construction. There is still rough and difficult terrain to be developed.

Youth workers need to understand that the teenage brain is still maturing, but it's rich with potential. Studies have shown that, when compared to adults, teenagers prefer physical activity, have less ability to plan in advance or practice sound judgment, demonstrate more risky and impulsive behaviors, and have minimal consideration for negative consequences.[3] This is why cell phone use and texting is so common among teenagers while they are driving. They put others in harm's way because they haven't thought carefully about the consequences of their behavior. Colorado just passed a law preventing teenagers (or anyone) from texting while driving. The state I live in recognized the risk and made a law against it.

Dr. Deborah Yurgelun-Todd of McLean Hospital in Belmont, Massachusetts, cites another study that suggests many teenagers are not able to correctly identify certain emotions expressed on another person's face. While virtually all adults could correctly identify a facial expression as reflecting "excitement," half of the adolescents saw the emotion "fear." This causes miscommunication and misinterpretation in relationships.[4] Have the young people you work with ever misinterpreted your words of counsel or teaching (not to mention their own "drama" in relationships with friends)? It could have been because of their development.

Research is just beginning to study the relationship between brain development and social networking sites such as Facebook. At the time this book was written, both Facebook and MySpace required members to be at least 13 years old, but many young people have admitted to lying about their ages in order to join the online phenomena. These sites have been linked to Internet addiction among adults, and some researchers worry that use of these sites by pre-adolescents (younger than 11 years old) could be damaging to the natural flow of child relationships and brain development.[5] Since Facebook has more than 350 million users, keeping young adolescents off this site is difficult. Similar concerns have been raised about excessive video game usage for teenagers. Those youth workers responsible for fifth and sixth graders in their ministries should heed these cautions.

It all starts in the brain. Youth workers need to be familiar with what is going on in teenage brains in order to disciple youth for Jesus Christ.

The brain immediately confronts us with its great complexity. The human brain weighs only three to four pounds but contains about 100 billion neurons. Although that extraordinary number is of the same order of magnitude as the number of stars in the Milky Way, it cannot account for the complexity of the brain.

—Gerald D. Fischbach, *Scientific American*

THE NEW ADOLESCENCE

In addition to brain development, we need to bring to light the changes in our understanding of adolescence. Some older adults believe the teenage experience hasn't changed much over the years. They often say, "It's just like when I was a teenager." Yet I tend to agree with researchers who believe outside forces and cultural changes have led our children and teenagers to be left behind. There has been what Dr. Chap Clark and others refer to as a "systematic abandonment" of our young people.[6] An often unintentional, yet profound desertion of adolescents is happening before our eyes—and this is an important area of discussion for those of us ministering to the next generation.

But before we go any further, it is helpful to define our terms. *Adolescence* is a relatively new word that came into use only within the last 60 to 100 years. It is derived from the Latin root word *adolescere,* meaning "to grow up." Most scholars consider this word to define those in the period between puberty and adulthood, the time when a child is growing up into a mature adult.[7] In the late nineteenth century, an American psychologist began to point out the significance of this middle phase between childhood and adulthood. Adolescents were not "big children" and were not "little adults"— they were in between.[8] This unique phase in maturity deserved special attention. A quick look at the public school system affirms that educators recognized the need for age-specific education because of developmental changes. This is why students usually attend different sites for elementary school, junior high or middle school, and high school.

For some in the church, there is no point in talking or thinking about adolescence. Because this word came out of the field of psychology, these people disregard it altogether. They argue that adolescence is never mentioned in the Bible, so there's no need for churches to pay any attention to it. We simply need to look to the Bible for answers.

I love the Scriptures and seek to root my life in the Word of God, but I still believe we need to understand areas of biology, psychiatry, philosophy, psychology, accounting, and others as they are informed and filtered through the sound doctrine of the biblical text. These fields are never mentioned in the Bible, but they are useful for us. Most of us wouldn't think of avoiding a particular doctor in a life-and-death situation because that doctor's field of expertise is not listed in the Bible. I think ignoring the insights of psychology and other social sciences is equally silly.

But some might say: *Wasn't Jesus "reasoning in the temple courts" at age 12 along with the religious leaders of the day? (Luke 2) If Jesus is our model, shouldn't we expect "adult things" from the teenagers in our ministries?* Well, yes we should have high expectations for the next generation, but we need to be very cautious about erasing the very real phase of growing up for adolescents.

I would argue that Jesus never went through a phase called *adolescence,* nor did any other Bible character. (Be careful using David or Timothy as examples of what teenagers should be like. They were probably adults in terms of their development.) Yes, Jesus was a teenager, but the culture of his time did not include this period of psychosocial development. Adolescence did not exist in biblical days, nor has it been present until the last 100 years. This is not because of low expectations, but biological and cultural influences.[9]

Think of the *Little House on the Prairie* books and television episodes. They depict a time before the Industrial Revolution had come on the American scene. In the 1800s, as in Jesus' day, children hit puberty and often were married within a year or two, at age 14 or 15. The concept of adolescence did not exist. One reason the biblical text does not include any account of Jesus' adolescent years is because he never experienced that phase of development. Like others of his time, Jesus went from child to adult practically overnight. This is why he could "reason" with the religious leaders in the temple courts at the age of 12.

Like a faithful missionary, those who care about helping the next generation come to love Jesus with all their hearts must sift everything through a sound biblical filter, but must also be informed by developmental and cultural realities of today. Otherwise, we'll miss the ministry boat with an intergenerational mindset (not to mention faithful youth ministry altogether).

I have great respect for the passion of Alex and Brett Harris, younger twin brothers of author and pastor Joshua Harris. These young men were home-schooled by two outstanding and loving parents and clearly have a faith that is more mature than most people their age. Their book *Do Hard Things*, written when the twins were just 19, does a great job of shining light on some of the heroic things teenagers have done. Yet I disagree with their chapter titled "The Myth of Adolescence."[10] In that chapter they blur the terms *teenager* and *adolescent.* These terms are not the same, as we've seen in this chapter. *Teenager* is simply an age bracket from 13 to 19, but *adolescence* is a psychosocial developmental term. One term counts the years since birth; the other is a recognized developmental stage. I celebrate that there are great young people who are stepping out in faith with God, but they are still traveling through the developmental phase called "adolescence" with physical and psychosocial implications. This distinct phase of life is well researched and taught by professors and practitioners at all levels in nearly every undergraduate and graduate program preparing ministers of the gospel to reach the next generation for Christ.

Psychology (and other social sciences) can offer significant insights that can benefit us in ministry and living. Just because a word like *adolescence* doesn't show up in the Bible, that does not mean we shouldn't take this specific phase of life seriously. Our ministries become more effective when we truly understand the way developing brains and cultural influences shape teenagers.

In fact, if the church did not recognize that adolescence is a unique stage of life and development, the specific field of youth ministry would not exist. There'd be no need for youth workers who focus on ministering to youth inside and outside the local church. But most churches have recognized the unique needs among this age demographic. Those of us who work with teens in ministry should be thankful it is a specific phase of development!

Consider what Dr. Chap Clark said nearly 10 years ago about the need for greater understanding among church leaders about the topic of adolescence:

> Theologians have only recently acknowledged the impact of adolescence on the church, missiological theory, or systematic theology. Although youth ministry has now become a staple in theological curriculum at all levels, there is almost no theological discussion—in print or otherwise—concerning adolescence. This trend may be waning, but as with many social realities, church leadership and thinking has a great deal of catching up to do.[11]

Although a decade has passed since Clark wrote these words, they are still true today. I remain concerned that pastors and church leaders on the front lines are not thinking and discussing at an increased level the implications of adolescence on ministry.

It is easy to swing too far in the other direction and start labeling youth ministry as bad—that we need to deconstruct youth ministry altogether. I think it is a natural part of adolescent development that teens want a place to call their own where they can seek out their faith by themselves. It is important that we help teens make their faith their own. Their own desire for that can be a positive reflection of that important adolescent development stage that has nothing to do with sin and rebellion against parents. I welcome adults of all ages to work with the teens, but I ask parents with teens in the youth group to honor their desire for the parents not to be there if that is how they feel. There is no need to create an unnecessary dichotomy.

—Didi, Youth Pastor

THE STARTING BLOCK

With an understanding of adolescence in place, let's turn our attention to the starting point of this phase of life. Studies show the average age for the onset of puberty in both boys and girls is becoming younger and younger. The normal range for the onset of puberty in girls can be as young as nine, while the normal range for boys begins at age ten.[12] In the nineteenth century, the average age for both boys and girls was around 14 or 15. Thus, the age for beginning adolescence is getting younger when marked by the biological factor of puberty.

In addition to the age of puberty getting younger, the psychosocial and psychological developmental processes have accelerated, too. Since these developmental changes are paralleling the physical aspects of adolescence, our mindset for ministry must also change. What was happening in youth ministry 40 years ago, because of the beginning age of adolescence and other social factors, will not work today.

For example, many churches are wrestling with what to do with fifth and sixth graders. These churches recognize that kids of this age need something beyond children's ministry. This is not a judgment on our ministry to children; it is a signal of the changing starting age of adolescence. The age is getting younger, thus we need to redesign our ministry to reach them.

But what about youth on the other end of the age spectrum?

THE FINISH LINE

While the starting line for adolescence is clearly getting younger based on biological factors, the ending of adolescence is more fluid. It is much more difficult to mark that point at which an adolescent officially becomes an adult. Some researchers have suggested that, "It starts in biology but ends in culture." Some people point to our society's standard age of 18. In my first book, written for youth workers, parents, and adolescent readers making the transition into college, I wrote:

> In the United States you're legally considered an adult on the day you turn 18. Once you're 18 a variety of privileges and responsibilities are yours: You can vote, own property, buy tobacco, marry without parental consent, be tried as an adult if you commit a crime, and even buy things from infomercials on late-night TV. So congratulations: If you're 18 or older, society says you're an adult. But is this really what adulthood is all about?[13]

Eighteen used to be the "right" age developmentally in part because that age corresponded with transitions such as graduation from high school and, often, marriage. But societal shifts have led to a lengthening of adolescence that now has shifted the proper age into the twenties. Today, research would point to the average age for coming out of adolescence and into adulthood to be the mid-twenties.[14] This is consistent with many factors, but especially brain development. Adolescence is indeed getting longer, but how do we know when an adolescent becomes an adult?

THE SIGNS

Many researchers and scholars believe that one way of measuring adolescence is through three critical life questions that adolescents typically wrestle with.[15] Sometimes, the adolescent's struggle with these questions is conscious, but many times it is subconscious. In other words, adolescents are not always consciously trying to figure all of this out, but rather, it is figuring *them* out. They are wrestling with these questions:

- Who am I? (Identity)
- Do my choices matter? (Autonomy)
- Where do I fit? (Belonging)

The name for the shift from adolescence to adulthood is "individuation." (You can see the connection to the word *individual*.) Carl Jung defines *individuation* in this way: "In general, it is the process by which individual beings are formed and differentiated; in particular, it is the development of the psychological individual as being distinct from the general, collective psychology. Individuation, therefore is a process of differentiation, having for its goal the development of the individual personality."[16]

Throughout the phase of adolescence, youth are developing their "individual personalities." With an understanding of this developmental process, leaders can walk beside the students in our care, helping them grow into mature Jesus-following adults.

David Elkind's view of rushing youth into adolescence is a form of abandonment. It's not letting children go through the process of being children. This forces them into this time of wondering who they are, what kind of power they have and where they fit…. We need to mobilize adults to care about the body of Christ.

—Dr. Chap Clark, *The Youthworker Journal Roundtable on Kids and Youth Culture*

GETTING MORE MATURE

Renowned psychologist Sigmund Freud once described growing in maturity as "loving and working." A mature adult is one who loves and allows himself or herself to be loved, and who can work productively with purpose and satisfaction. Many adolescents are not yet fully capable of loving and working in these ways. When children and adolescents are expected to speak a certain way, dress a certain way, and think a certain way so they seem more "adult-like," they are really being forced to perform on the stage of the adult world. Such behavior is not genuine, but a skill some youth have learned in order to cope with the pressure. They are actors on the movie screen of life development, putting on different "selves" to experiment. They are not ready for adulthood, yet some act like they are ready because they've been told (sometimes unintentionally, other times deliberately) that they need to "grow up fast."

Yet children and adolescents need time to grow, to learn, and to develop on a natural timeline. This includes their faith walk with Jesus. As youth workers, parents, and other caring adults journey alongside adolescents, we need to help them discover biblically rooted answers to the developmental questions of Identity, Autonomy, and Belonging. The Bible offers sound answers to these developmental questions, and we Christian adults are seeking to live out these answers. If we take on a mindset for ministry that is intergenerational, we recognize that every adolescent is a uniquely designed masterpiece in the making—and we all have roles to play in helping our youth become all that God wants them to be.

In our current culture, the period of adolescence can extend for 15 years or more. We need to take this phase of life seriously. Every adolescent was built for community with older adults, peer friends, and children who are younger. In the context of intergenerational connections in the local church, adolescents need to be discipled on their way to becoming mature Jesus-following adults.

FIGHT FOR IDENTITY

Many cultural forces are battling to shape adolescent identities. If the church does not take seriously the identity development in adolescents, we will lose many to the world. One of the primary forces shaping young people today is consumerism.

Kit Yarrow, a consumer psychologist at Golden Gate University in San Francisco, has been studying adolescent shopping habits for years. Journalist Chris O'Brien interviewed Yarrow one day at a favorite teenage hangout: The mall. Yarrow notes, "It's not just the amount of shopping by this generation that's unique, but the reasons behind it." O'Brien's article goes on to explain that buying stuff is one way Generation Y (born in the late 1970s to the 1990s, also called Millennials) has learned to express itself. It's not so much about accumulating large amounts of stuff or declaring one's financial status (as was the case with baby boomers). Rather, for Generation Y shopping is a new form of self-expression. Yarrow says, "Stuff is a natural, easy way to say who you are."[17]

Youth workers and other caring adults need to help adolescents find their identity from a different source. We need to help youth discover that who they are is not determined by the stuff they own their experiences of collecting stuff, but by a real, loving God.

No growing up occurs if there is nothing to grow up to. Without the adult connection, adolescence becomes a neverland, a Mall of Lost Children.

—Lance Morrow, "The Boys and the Bees" (*Time Magazine*)

ANONYMOUS ADOLESCENTS

Many teens have high levels of stress because they feel isolated and unknown. I will never forget what happened one Sunday morning in a church where I was directing the high school youth program. As we were ushering (okay, maybe herding) all the students into the designated youth room, I noticed three guys sitting in the hallway with their backs against the wall. I walked up and introduced myself, asked their names, and reached out my hand to high-five them in a friendly (a.k.a. cool) gesture. "Come inside," I said. "We were just getting started."

It did not go well.

They ignored me when I spoke to them. They did not offer their names (or high-fives). Smiles came across their faces as they looked at one another, and I began to feel the same way I used to feel as a kid when I'd get picked last for the neighborhood football game. Before I knew what had happened, they jumped up and ran down the hallway laughing, headed out the exit door and into the parking lot, got into their car, and drove away. *What just happened?* I thought to myself. *Was it something I said?* (I know I wore deodorant that day!) *Was the high-five too much?* They wanted nothing to do with me.

Later I compared notes with other adults on our youth team, and they'd had similar experiences with the same three guys. "No way," I said. None of us knew their names, where they lived, what grade they were in, or the school they attended. I even asked other students.

They were anonymous.

Now, this might be an unusual group of guys, but I think there is something in this story that is real for many adolescents today. They don't want any significant contact with adults. They prefer to remain partially or fully anonymous because it is safer that way. They do not believe adults really understand or care about them. Many adults seem scary, inauthentic, and just not safe to be around emotionally.

Years ago, our youth group spent a weekend in the mountains of Colorado for a retreat. On Saturday afternoon I got to relax with the youth around a warm fireplace. I decided to take advantage of the time with these high school students and ask them some questions. After some small talk, I asked, "Do you guys think adults understand you?"

I was amazed by the conversation that flowed for the next couple of hours. It was like a dam had broken. These students immediately and unanimously agreed that adults did not really understand them. "Why not?" I asked.

"They don't understand that we are under real pressure," one said. "There is stress at school, with sports, and with friends." said another. "Our stress is as big as our parents' stress at work and home." Other kids said, "My parents and other adults don't understand that we are serious about our faith, and that it is real."

I learned some valuable lessons that weekend that I've carried with me ever since. My conversation with those kids matches the findings of researchers and educators around the country. Beneath the surface, most youth feel alone, abandoned, and misunderstood.

While writing this chapter in a coffee shop one afternoon, I overheard some middle school girls who'd stopped in after school. They were talking openly about who was having sex with whom, gossiping about friends, sharing thoughts about teachers at school, and slamming their parents (after one girl received a cell phone call from her mom). They were in their own world, and they did not want to be disturbed by an outside adult.

Such conversations offer us a glimpse of what researchers are finding behind the curtain to the underground world of adolescents.[18] Dr. Chap Clark calls it the "world beneath"—a place where loneliness and darkness dwells. On the surface, students seem happy, joyful, and unaffected by the stress around them, but in reality they are putting on different "selves" to cope with an adult world where they truly believe they are not understood. Yet they have created an "underground world" where they negotiate rules with diverse groups of friends. They do not care as much about "being popular" as being "understood"—which helps them feel safe and secure.

Whether at local hangouts like coffee shops and the mall or through the virtual world offered by social networking sites, students are finding places away from adults. They tend to be in isolated clusters of friendships of five or six youth of the same gender. Kids come to the "adult world" only when they are required to appear in places such as school, athletic teams, jobs, church, and other places in culture.

For the most part, caring adults have a difficult time "heading down" to meet teenagers "where they are." Often, the best we can pray for is to catch them in our spheres of influence and, with grace and love, "sit on the stairs" of the underground world. Over time, if we truly show we are there for them, adolescents might begin to open up to caring adults.

Take a look at the picture below of the "underground world":

THE UNDERGROUND ADOLESCENT WORLD

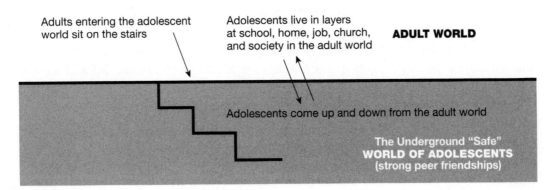

Adults entering the adolescent world sit on the stairs

Adolescents live in layers at school, home, job, church, and society in the adult world

ADULT WORLD

Adolescents come up and down from the adult world

The Underground "Safe"
WORLD OF ADOLESCENTS
(strong peer friendships)

NEGLECTED

Most of us got involved in youth work because we felt God calling us to connect with youth, to care about them, and to help them come to know and love Jesus Christ. And some teens are building connections with adults who can help them find a deeper faith. Most likely these are the youth who are already on their way in the process of *individuation*.

But many other students feel alone—and that's often because they *really* are alone. Instead of neighborhoods filled with front porch conversations, as a society we've headed to the back decks of isolation. I grew up in a small town in Michigan where very few people had fences surrounding their property. In my upper elementary and teenage school years, I remember running the neighborhood with my friends, playing all sorts of games in every yard and by creeks. All the students in the neighborhood would suddenly appear from their homes whenever a ball was present. There seemed to be this invisible line of communication between the adults in the three-block area near my house. We kids were in and out of every home, taking drink breaks, resting, and having conversations with adults.

Today, I live in the Denver area where the neighborhoods are divided by subdivisions and fence lines. Fences are up, garage doors are down, and all is quiet most of the time. Kids have less proactive communication with adults, and it is a larger chore for youth to spend time together outside of their bedrooms or loitering at a nearby park. Youth seem to want to get as far away from adults as possible. I spoke with a twenty-something friend the other day who shared with me that as a child and teenager he spent hours alone in his bedroom playing video games because he wanted to. It was safe. This is heartbreaking, but I believe the norm for many adolescents.

Schools have also changed in ways that limit close connections between youth and adults. Many classrooms today have 30 or more students in them. This often leaves very little opportunity for individual students to connect with their teachers. Author and pastor Mark DeVries makes the point, "A growing number of very committed teachers have a tremendous impact on the values of their students. But as a general rule, teachers simply don't have the time for nondirective conversations with their students. The majority of the time teenagers spend in school is dedicated to isolated work alone and periodically with peers, but seldom in meaningful conversation with adults."[19] This is a tragedy.

Many youth spend their weekend hanging out with friends and without any adults around. As a result, the teenage party scene is alive and well, and alcohol use and all forms of sexual behavior are seen as normal. Even junior high students who have not fully developed physically or psychosocially are left alone in homes and "experimenting" with their sexuality. Many adults are oblivious to what is happening, but some don't mind thinking it is just a phase or worse, "normal."

Probably the most devastating place of abandonment is within families. There is no doubt teenagers spend less time with their parents or guardians today than at any other time in history. In previous generations, families would eat together, work together, and have fun together. Today, it's far more common for everybody to go their separate ways during the day—and the same happens at night in most families. In general, research shows that most adolescents want better relationships with their parents. They might put up "smoke screens" that make it appear they want parents and other adults to keep their distance, but deep down in their souls they know that a better relationship with their parents is what they were created to experience.[20] We will explore more about family dynamics in the next chapter.

OUR TURF

There is one other place where youth often feel isolated and abandoned—and this is the one that may be the hardest for us youth workers to think and talk about. Have our churches—have we—done the same thing to our adolescents? Have we built walls of isolation around our youth? We might hope that churches would do a better job than neighborhoods, schools, and perhaps even some families in providing youth with life-shaping relationships with older adults. But sadly, church is one of the places where teenagers are most separated from adults. We built separate youth ministry buildings with separate office spaces for the staff. We set up youth programming apart from the rest of the church. We built separate youth Sunday school classes, youth worship teams, youth-led small groups, youth evangelism strategies, youth choirs, youth conferences, youth fundraisers, and, well, youth ministries. For the most part, even in the main worship services of church, the youth sit together (if they are present) and the adults sit together. There is separation.

"Success" in youth ministry has historically been measured by the number of kids who show up to programs and events, not by the integration and assimilation of our youth into the body of Christ before and after high school graduation. At most, ministry to adolescents is considered a "limb" of the church (as are most other ministries), when it should be the "lungs" that breathe new life into the intergenerational congregation of believers.

We need to change our goals and mindset for ministry. There are far worse things that can happen than to have bad and boring programming. Not intentionally connecting adolescents with Jesus-following adults and thus helping them become excited about the local church as a whole leaves us in dangerous quicksand in the future.

HURRIED AND HURT

Maybe this news is no surprise to the average youth worker, pastor, or parent, but I believe it should be a wake-up call that demands that we change our mindset for ministry. Too many adolescents feel alone and abandoned in neighborhoods, families, schools, and even in the church. Teenagers are rushed to grow up much faster than they did just 10 or 20 years ago, and this is causing deep and lasting hurt.

Today's teenagers are faced with tremendous pressure to be "adult-like" in their thinking and actions. Ironically, even though all social researchers agree that adolescence is a distinct phase of life, today's young people still face overwhelming stress and rising expectations from parents and other adults. It is no wonder that by the time they reach their teenage years, many youth want their independence so badly that they begin to take on negative "adult" behaviors such as smoking, having sex, drinking, or reckless driving. When teens are expected to shoulder adult responsibilities such as making car payments, grocery shopping, caring for younger siblings, and the like, it is difficult for them to grow up at a healthy developmental pace. Adults are tricked into thinking that maturity on the outside means maturity on the inside.

Marketers have noticed the same changes in the rate at which adolescents are expected to mature—and they know there's money coming from this research. Reflecting on adolescent shopping habits, one researcher writes, "On the downside, it is an anxious generation, worried that being told they can do everything, they are actually expected to do it. They mature much more slowly. And they have set the bar high in terms of their jobs and relationships. The result is a tremendous amount of stress. Many of Generation Y's surveyed said shopping provided a 'mental vacation.'"[21] Caring adults need to understand that the pressure on our youth is rising. Unless we slow down the maturity speed, we will cause more unnatural stress for adolescents.

RAISING THE BAR

It is important to acknowledge that seeking to limit the pressure on our youth does not mean we should lower our standards regarding Christian belief and practice in an adolescent's life. Jesus' words about discipleship still ring true. On the contrary, we must continue (or start) teaching the truths of Scripture with passion, while understanding adolescence is a distinct life phase. Even more than using our words to speak about biblical principles to adolescents, youth workers and other caring adults need to *live out* the values of Scripture in front of the next generation.

This is one area where I definitely do agree with what the Harris brothers wrote in their book *Do Hard Things*. I join the Harrises in their belief that we need to keep raising the bar high for the coming generations. Yet I think we have to realize that expecting adolescents to "get it fully" or to "be fully adult" is not realistic because of the specific developmental phase of life they are encountering. If we do not recognize this, we will contribute to their growing up too fast.

We understand this reality with younger children. Parents don't expect a three-month-old infant to know how to walk and talk. We know these milestones will come in time. In the meantime, we enjoy, love, and care for children where they are. When a child reaches 10 to 12 months, many parents let the child grab their fingers as he or she attempts to stand and eventually go fully mobile. Again, we celebrate these developmental and literal steps. The same is true in every stage of development. Infancy turns to childhood, which turns to adolescence, and finally adulthood. So keep the bar high, but do so with a realistic pace and expectations of teenage discipleship.

I have seen hundreds of youth ministry programs, consulted with several dozen churches and parachurch groups, and interacted with thousands of youth ministry leaders and students over the course of my life. Here's something I have learned: Abandonment is not limited to "secular" programs and institutions but is alive and well in the systems and structures of the church. Youth ministry is often concerned with numerical growth, superficial and instant response, and active attendance, making it more about the ministry than about the individual [students]. This is a recipe for abandonment.

—Dr. Chap Clark, *When Kids Hurt*

BIGGER AND BROADER GOALS

What I have described in this chapter is no small matter. With the lengthening of adolescence, challenges of abandonment and isolation, stress on families, and the pressure churches feel to reach the next generation, big and broad goals must be established. In the final chapter of this book, we will attempt to bring together the goals that define this new approach for ministry.

An intergenerational mindset for ministry requires more than just making sure teenagers attend church youth events each week. Just as the African proverb reminds us, "It takes a village to raise a child," it takes a church to raise a teenager into full Christian maturity. None of us can do it alone. No youth worker or parents can do it alone. It takes an entire church to give students the attention they need to become mature Jesus-following adults.

In his 1997 book, *All Kids Are Our Kids*, Peter Benson, president of the Search Institute, described what was happening as a result of the slowing down in adolescent development.[22] He wrote, "For the first time in the history of this country, young people are *less* healthy and *less* prepared to take their places in society than were their parents. And this is happening at a time when our society is more complex, more challenging and more competitive than ever before."[23] In the decade since Benson's book was written, things have only gotten worse. I think Benson's words are a gross understatement for what adolescents face today in our society.

Based on its extensive research in the field of adolescent development, Benson and the Search Institute have established a list of 40 developmental assets that are valuable for youth ages 12 to 18 years old.[24] Because of the lengthening of adolescence, as covered in our earlier discussion, I'd suggest that this list of assets is important for youth older than age 18 as well. Certainly late adolescents need many of these assets in order to become fully mature adults.

Benson divides assets into those that are *external* to youth and those that are *internal,* and he also groups the key assets into a number of different subcategories.[25] These assets are worth meditating on as we consider an intergenerational approach to ministry that reaches the whole adolescent.

THE 40 DEVELOPMENTAL ASSETS

EXTERNAL ASSETS:

Support: The support assets are those experiences that communicate love, affirmation, and acceptance.

- Family Support
- Positive Family Communication
- Other Adult Relationships
- Caring Neighborhood
- Caring School Climate
- Parent Involved in Schooling

Empowerment: The empowerment assets are those experiences that make youth feel valued and valuable. Adolescents grow up feeling respected and supported when this is in place. These are balanced with boundaries.

- Community Values Youth
- Youth as Resources
- Service to Others
- Safety

Boundaries and Expectations: These assets involve giving clear signals about what is expected, what is approved and celebrated, and what deserves censure.

- Family Boundaries
- School Boundaries
- Neighborhood Boundaries

- Adult Role Models
- Positive Peer Influenc
- High Expectations

Constructive Use of Time: Through organizations and programs, these assets are developed. This requires older adults to connect with adolescents helping them work on skills, abilities, and gift development.

- Creative Opportunities
- Youth Programs
- Religious Community
- Time at Home

INTERNAL ASSETS:

Commitment to Learning: Learning assets are personal qualities and behaviors that are conducive to intellectual growth.

- Achievement Motivation
- School Engagement
- Homework
- Bonding to School
- Reading for Pleasure

Positive Values: Positive value assets are foundational because they form personal character, shape choices, and enable youth to practice moral restraint.

- Caring
- Equality and Social Justice
- Integrity
- Honesty
- Responsibility
- Restraint

Social Competencies: Social competency assets are often emphasized in alcohol- and drug-prevention programs. The peaceful conflict resolution asset is one that is often taught in schools, but can be taught in ministry settings as well.

- Planning and Decision Making
- Interpersonal Competence
- Cultural Competence

- Resistance Skills
- Peaceful Conflict Resolution

Positive Identity: Positive identity assets are those that keep young people from becoming powerless victims without a sense of initiative, direction, and purpose.

- Personal Power
- Self-Esteem
- Sense of Purpose
- Positive View of Personal Future

Benson contends that as more of these assets are found in a community, fewer youth become involved in at-risk behaviors, and more youth engage in positive behaviors like feeling compassion for others, acting like leaders, succeeding in school, developing healthy lifestyles, and showing the resiliency needed to come back from difficult situations.

Developing these assets in our youth requires that churches bring a different kind of thinking to ministry. Take another look at the list. Notice how many of these assets are related to the role of older adults in the lives of youth. Did you spot *any* that do not involve young people's relationships to adults in one way or another? Certainly, the external assets need adult interaction, and most of the internal assets could be more fully developed with adults spending more time around the next generation. (Certainly, the idea of individuation with its three aspects of Identity, Autonomy, and Belonging is reflected in this internal list of assets.) How much more effective would ministry to the next generation be if mature Jesus-following adults were surrounding all the adolescents in our care?

Here is the principle that I believe every youth worker must take to heart for effective intergenerational ministry: *The more adults youth workers recruit and train in ministry to surround every individual adolescent, the better chance these adolescents will have to become mature Jesus-following adults.* Churches that care deeply about the next generation growing up to become mature followers of Christ need to take seriously the development of these 40 assets. This requires a firm commitment to God and to the future of the church. It requires a body of believers working together to reach every adolescent in our care. This requires more than the youth pastor. It requires the whole tribe—the body of Christ. Together, we must commit to living out the full message of the gospel in ways that will speak to the youth in our care.

It also requires that we get on the same page about our message. We need not just community convergence but community *congruence.* We need unity in our message. If we are sending mixed signals to our youth, we are in trouble. The church must strive to remove inconsistencies and hypocrisy in programs, services, and the home.[26] Caring adults and youth workers must create and cultivate the same biblically rooted message in all aspects of our curriculum and programming. The 40 Developmental Assets will help move us forward with practical benchmarks and environments for effective intergenerational ministry to youth.

Keeping community convergence and congruence in mind, our churches must create opportunities for adolescents and adults to know God and make him known to a surrounding community. We must join hands with one another and with schools and other community services to help develop healthy and God-honoring youth and young adults. The future of the local church depends on it.

CONTINUE THE CONVERSATION

1. How does understanding adolescent brain development affect how you teach the Bible to young people?
2. Why is it helpful in ministry to be aware of the development of adolescents?
3. How do the concepts of Identity, Autonomy, and Belonging shape your ministry?
4. What has been your experience with the "underground adolescent world"?
5. How could you use the list of external and internal assets of development in your ministry to the next generation?

3
GOING INSIDE THE WALLS

LOOKING AT TODAY'S FAMILY

The best way to keep teens at home is to make the home atmosphere pleasant, and let the air out of the tires.

—Dorothy Parker

For most Christian teenagers, Sunday school and youth group have become a substitute for spiritual training in the home. Interestingly enough, the Sunday-school movement itself began as an outreach to *unchurched* poor children. Its founders never intended for it to take over the role of Christian parents.

—Mark DeVries

Adolescence is something that happens to a family, not just an individual.

—Sarah Silberstein Swartz

Fathers, do not exasperate your children; instead, bring them up in the training and instruction of the Lord.

—Paul in Ephesians 6:4

Many places in our current culture are beat up, but none more so than the contemporary family. It is bruised and broken. So many families are fragmented. Although many parents are involved in the lives of their teenagers, too many others are stressed out and removed. At a time when adolescents need their parents the most, far too many parents are absent or disconnected.

We tend to assume kids don't think too of[f] parents have on their lives. But many studies show th.. ...agers want more time with their parents because they recognize the significance of having their parents involved in their lives. In one study, when teens were asked what one thing makes them most happy, teens mentioned spending time with family more than any other answer. About three-quarters (73 percent) said their relationship with their parents makes them happy. With all the focus on the way youth are shaped by their friends and peers, some of us may find it surprising that relationships with family were mentioned more often and viewed as more significant than relationships with friends.[1]

Many homes experience intense conflict during the adolescent years. When I talk to parents of teens or overhear conversations in coffee shops and around the local church about the topic of raising teenagers, conflict seems to be the one common factor. Conflict is not always bad, but if a high level of conflict persists, it can cause great difficulty in the relationship between adolescent and parent.[2] But the overwhelming research points to the importance of the parents' relationship to their teenager during adolescence. In one study, when teens were asked if they could have one wish granted, 48 percent wished for more time with their families.[3] Teenagers also recognize the key role parents have in shaping their lives. In George Barna's *Third Millennium Teens* report, 78 percent of teens said their parents had a lot of influence over them.[4]

Unfortunately, work, other priorities, and the breakdown of families means many young people don't spend enough quality time with their parents. The breakup of parents continues to be a huge issue in the lives of many adolescents. Divorce is a public matter with deep private hurt. Rather than being raised by two parents in a single household, divorce means many teens are raised by a single parent, or are shuttled frequently from one parent's home to another. With this instability comes an inconsistent pattern of raising the teenager. Boundaries are different. Rules become confusing. Some teenagers are raised without any parental influence whatsoever. Needless to say, this causes a tremendous amount of confusion, hurt, and disillusion for many who are growing up in these homes.

In addition to the increased number of single-parent and other nontraditional families, most families are moving at warp speed. With students involved in extracurricular activities, traveling sports teams, church functions, homework pressures, and jobs, family schedules are out of control. Parents find themselves wanting to please their teenagers by allowing them to participate in as many activities as possible (and spending lots of money to do so). Many times this adds stress because there are no boundaries in the teen's life. This just adds to the bumps and bruises received while heading through adolescence.

…body has ever before asked the nuclear family to live all by itself …n a box the way we do. With no relatives, no support, we've put it in an impossible situation.

—Margaret Mead

This is not a pretty picture of teenagers and families. There are many wonderful things happening in the lives of adolescents today, and some research shows that relationships between adolescents and parents can be good, especially in families where parents take a proactive role in their child's spiritual life and help nurture the child's involvement with the church. But a realistic view of students and families shows far too many bruised and broken households. We need to help pick up the pieces with God's help and move into the future with powerful confidence.

Thankfully, not all the news is bad for families. Consider the following words from Richard Lerner, a professor at Tufts University:

> Research shows that most young people go through adolescence having good relationships with their parents, adopting attitudes and values consistent with their parents' and end up getting out of the adolescent period and becoming good citizens. This shouldn't be news—but it is, largely because of widespread misunderstanding of what happens during the teen years. It's a time of transition, just like the first year of parenthood or menopause. And although there are dramatic hormonal and physical changes during this period, catastrophe is certainly not preordained. A lot depends on youngsters' innate natures combined with the emotional and social support they get from the adults around them. In other words, parents do matter.

THE THEOLOGY OF PARENTING

Parenting was God's idea, and it lands on the human scene in the first few pages of the Bible when Adam and Eve are given the command to "multiply." In the Old Testament, God stresses the importance of families passing on the faith: "These commandments that I give you today are to be on your hearts. Impress them on your children. Talk about them when you sit at home and when you walk along the road, when you lie down and when you get up" (Deuteronomy 6:6–7). The care of parents and community is intended to help the next generation learn to "love the Lord your God with all your heart and with all your soul and with all your mind"—what Jesus called the Greatest Commandment. (See Deuteronomy 6:5, Matthew 22:37.)

The Bible stresses the role of parents in the spiritual training of an adolescent. Paul had strong words for fathers (as well as mothers) in the church in Ephesus: "Fathers, do not exasperate your children; instead, bring them up in the training and instruction of the Lord" (Ephesians 6:4). In Colossians parents are similarly urged to provide spiritual nurture in the home while being careful not to "exasperate" or "embitter" their children (Colossians 3:21). Parents are called to love and care for their children following the model of God who becomes "father to the fatherless" (Psalm 68:5). The Father in heaven has compassion on all his children and will work in and through even the most difficult family situations for his glory (Psalm 103:13).

Our loyalty to the church is not a tool for escaping responsibility at home. Rather, our connectedness to the community of faith is the very thing that should hold us accountable for our faithfulness to family, work and church.

—Mark DeVries, *Family-Based Youth Ministry*

As youth workers, we must do our best to help young people understand and rely on the promises and instructions of Scripture, while not trying to replace the role of parents in the lives of adolescents. Ultimately, it is the parents' job to "train a child in the way he should go" (Proverbs 22:6 NIV), not the job of the church youth director or volunteer leader. Youth workers, volunteers, and the entire church community must come alongside parents in partnership and help youth grow in their love of God and neighbor (Matthew 22:34–40).

When you look at your life, the greatest happinesses are family happinesses.

—Dr. Joyce Brothers

A FIRE HYDRANT OF STATS

Have you tried to drink water from a wide-open fire hydrant? Me neither, but I imagine it'd be pretty overwhelming! I'd like to overwhelm you with the evidence regarding the importance of parents in the lives of adolescents. Maybe you don't need reminding about this, but I think it is healthy for us to see what is at stake. Without a proper understanding of the influence of the family, we might not be inclined to change our minds toward intergenerational ministry. Let's avoid this temptation by looking at the evidence—and by sharing it in training times with volunteers, parents, and pastors.

George Barna and the Barna Group have done a great deal of research regarding parents and families. I think Barna is right on when he says this about church leaders:

> Many church leaders talk about the importance of the family, but in practice they have written off the family as an agency of spiritual influence. Their assumption is that if the family (including teenagers) is going to be influenced, it is the organized church that will do the influencing, primarily through its events—worship services, classes, special events, etc. This philosophy causes the impetus behind youth ministry to be fixing what is broken—that is, to substitute the efforts of the church for those of parents since most of the latter do not provide the spiritual direction and accountability that their children need. But there is a procedural problem here: Kids take their cues from their family, not from their youth ministers. God's plan was for the church to support the family, and for the family to be the front-line of ministry within the home. Teenagers may glean some truths and principles from youth leaders, but the greatest influence in their lives will remain their parents.[5]

Barna is right. Our thinking must change. Our vision must change. Our starting point must change. We need a new mindset that focuses on the family as the primary spiritual influence in an adolescent's life.

I know a lot of youth pastors who would say they agree with this idea of families being important, but when it comes to their actual programming, they think and plan very differently—with church youth programs on one side and parents on the other side. In effect, they tell parents, "I will take your teenagers for a few hours of the week, and you take them for the other time—and never shall our paths cross." This approach needs to change.

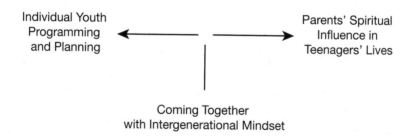

Individual Youth Programming and Planning ← → Parents' Spiritual Influence in Teenagers' Lives

Coming Together with Intergenerational Mindset

The typical youth pastor thinks about teenagers and how the church can reach and minister to them. We're always thinking about what kinds of events, curriculum, programs, and outreach can make a difference among the youth God has placed in our care. Yet parents and families are often far down the list of priorities. Why is this? We have a fantastic resource and biblical model right under our noses, but we are not partnering with parents in an intergenerational mindset.

Maybe churches should think more like hospitals at times.

We recognize the value of every person and are guided by our commitment to excellence and leadership. We demonstrate this by: Providing exemplary physical, emotional and spiritual care for each of our patients and their families.

—**Mission Statement of St. Michael's Hospital, Ontario, Canada**

EGO BUSTER FOR YOUTH WORKERS

Maybe it has something to do with our egos. We want to make a difference for Christ in the lives of kids—that's the whole reason we started working with youth in the first place. So it's tough for us to admit that we youth workers, no matter how faithful we might be, are not the ones who have the most influence in the lives of most of the young people in our ministries.

Sometimes I need someone to put me in my proper place. As soon as I think I am bigger than life, God will bring something along to humble me. It doesn't always feel good, but it is needed. For example, consider the results of a survey conducted by Weekly Reader Research from the American Bible Society. A survey of 1,100 teens, ages 12 to 18, found that 67.7 percent believe parents are the most important role models in today's society. Parents were followed by teachers and coaches at 40.6 percent. Siblings were close behind at 40.4 percent. Religious leaders came in way down the list, at 18.7 percent.[6] *Ouch!*

Another survey by the Center for Youth and Family Ministry looked specifically at teenagers involved with church youth programs. When these high school seniors were asked who their sources of support are, parents were the primary source of support. Coming in next were youth group leaders, then peers from outside of the youth group, then peers from within the youth group, and then other adults in the church.[7] (Does it surprise you that friends outside the church were cited as a source of support more often than friends *inside* the church youth group?) But again, the parents topped the list, cited more often than both youth pastors and other church-related adults. *Another ouch!*

The mega company, Virgin Mobile, says that teens named parents as their chief role models coming in at 71 percent. The next role model named at a distant 40 percent was the public school teacher.[8] (This research also pointed out that this is the first generation to share the same music tastes as their parents.) *Ouch again!*

To us, family means putting your arms around each other and being there.

—Barbara Bush

Did you know that parents also have the greatest influence on teenagers' dating relationships—even more than their friends do? One study found that 35 percent of teenagers said their parents were the biggest influence on their dating choices. Friends came in at 28 percent. Religious leaders were cited at only 3 percent. Perhaps even more amazing is the fact that 67 percent of girls in the study and 62 percent of guys said they found it easy to talk to their parents about relationships.[9] The media and other sources tend to portray a very different story of parent and teenage relationships. It should both humble and excite us youth workers to realize we are not the greatest influences on a teen's dating relationship. The greatest influence is not the youth pastor. It's not even the volunteer who has built such great relationships with the girls in her small group. It is parents. Amazing. *A final ouch!*

Maybe this information makes you uneasy. You might have thought you were the person who has the greatest spiritual impact on the teenagers in your youth group. You aren't. And I believe that's good news for youth workers. Parents are still perceived by most teenagers as primary role models and positive influences. We youth workers need to swallow a humility pill and partner with this God-given resource. Parents are supposed to have this kind of impact. Let's cheer them on!

The family. We were a strange little band of characters trudging through life sharing diseases and toothpaste, coveting one another's desserts, hiding shampoo, borrowing money, locking each other out of our rooms, inflicting pain and kissing to heal it in the same instant, loving, laughing, defending, and trying to figure out the common thread that bound us all together.

—Erma Bombeck, *Family—The Ties That Bind ... and Gag!*

TEENAGE TIME WITH PARENTS

Did you know that most teenagers love spending time with their parents? Talk-show mayhem and media reports do not portray this reality. Most onlookers probably think adolescents dislike their parents. Even parents themselves often have a very negative perspective on the next generation. I have overheard so many conversations in coffee shops where parents express frustration about their teenage sons and daughters. These parents may not believe their teenage children value these relationships, but they do.

We've seen that adolescence is a developmental phase where the individual is straining for independence and autonomy. Their outward smoke screen of "rebellion" is really not what is happening on the inside. Most teens love their parents and intuitively understand the influence parents have on their lives. A survey by the National Campaign to Prevent Teen and Unplanned Pregnancy found that teenagers ages 15 to 17 say they enjoy spending time with their mother (79 percent) and father (76 percent).[10] Another study found that the majority of early adolescents (ages 10 to 12) look to mom and dad as their role models.[11]

The roots of misconceptions about teenagers go back to the way psychologists framed the field of adolescent development a century ago. They were primarily looking for explanations of why things went wrong. Before long, the idea that this phase was a period of storm and stress made its way into the popular consciousness. But in the last 15 years, developmental scientists have begun to re-examine these assumptions. Instead of focusing on kids who battle their way through the teen years, they're studying the dynamics of success.[12]

— Barbara Kantrowitz

PARENTS ARE THE STRONGEST INFLUENCE

Time and time again, research points to the powerful influence of parents in adolescents' lives. It should come as no surprise that parents have a large impact on fostering positive self-esteem in girls. Jess Weiner of the Dove Self-Esteem Fund expressed, "The good news is that if parents and other role models are willing to create a steady conversation of encouragement, honesty, and openness, it can definitely help girls gain confidence and reach their full potential."[13]

One interesting research project done by the Mayo Clinic set out to study the root causes of teenagers' high-risk behaviors. More than 90,000 junior and senior high students were asked to fill out questionnaires anonymously. Those questionnaires were followed by more than 12,000 face-to-face interviews. The questions were geared toward mental and emotional distress, drug and alcohol abuse, sexual involvement, and violent behavior. The conclusion was, "The most effective way to protect young people from unhealthy or dangerous behaviors is for parents to be involved in their lives."[14] Teenagers who reported a strong connection with their parents were less likely to engage in these negative behaviors. Another study found similar results: Those teens who spend significant time with their parents, talk with them frequently, and feel close to them are much less likely to develop problems with alcohol or use drugs.[15] How about that?

Despite media portrayals to the contrary, most teenagers actually want to spend more time with their parents. One online survey of 1,250 adults and teens revealed that 67 percent of teens say they actually want to spend more time with their parents.[16] Just a few years ago a survey revealed that 9 out of 10 teens say they're "close" to their parents; 75 percent say "they like to do things with their family", and 59 percent say family dinners are "in."[17]

The family should be a closely knit group. The home should be a self-contained shelter of security; a kind of school where life's basic lessons are taught; and a kind of church where God is honored; a place where wholesome recreation and simple pleasures are enjoyed.

—Billy Graham

Parents also have a great deal of influence on their teenagers when it comes to spiritual matters. In one study 68 percent of teens ages 13 to 18 said they discuss religion with their families. The same percentage of teens said their religious views were similar to those of their parents.[18] Barna's research found that, among teenagers who declared themselves born-again Christians, 82 percent said their parents have been good role models of how to be a person of strong and meaningful faith.[19] According to the data collected for the College Transition Project, one of the most significant differences parents can make in the faith of their teenager is through their discussions. Teenagers who report talking to parents about both their own faith and the faith of their parents feel more supported by God.[20]

As those trained in theology, culture, and adolescent development, youth leaders can come alongside parents by helping them have a clear understanding of the gospel and training them to share it with their teenagers. (We'll discuss this more in the chapter on evangelism.) In short, as Rick Lawrence of Group Publishing has said, "If you want to impact your teenagers deeply for Christ, to draw kids more deeply into a Jesus-centered lifestyle, few things are more important than impacting their parents."[21] Recognizing that parents have the greatest influence on a teenager's spiritual growth, our job as youth workers is to come alongside and fan the flames of relationship and spiritual growth with both parents and adolescents.

EVEN YOUNG ADULTS . . .

We might assume that the importance of parental influence drops off significantly as young people end their teenage years. But this is not the case. In recent years, while I've been continuing to oversee staff who work directly with junior high and senior high ministries, I've been working with college and career twentysomethings in the local church. My experience is that young adult ministries have become the "new youth ministries." As we discussed in the previous chapter, the lengthening of adolescence means that young people in this age group are still in late adolescence. And in this stage, the task of nurturing and supporting relationships between young adults and their parents remains important.

When a group of researchers who had been studying the twentysomething generation were asked what most surprised them or challenged their stereotypes about the young people they'd studied, they reported that it was the relationships these young adults had with their parents.[22] Almost half of all young adults talk to their parents every day on the telephone (not to mention email, text messaging, and, for some, instant messaging). Young people today seem to have a much more open relationship with their parents than previous generations have had. Marketers, employers, and Gen Nexters all seem to agree that the parent-child relationship has changed. This generation is characterized by "helicopter parents" who have encouraged their children to follow their dreams and assured them they can be whatever they want to be when they grow up. Certainly this can have positive and negative effects for young adults who grew up with safety first and "everyone is a winner" in all areas of their lives. But the good news is that parents and young adults remain closely connected.

In one online study of more than 1,500 adolescents ages 13 to 24, researchers reported the following: "Millennials exhibit strong familial relationships and bonds.

Seven in ten are 'satisfied' with their family life, three out of four place a high degree of importance on being close to their parents and siblings. Interestingly the oldest segment of late adolescents, 22–24-year-olds, are most satisfied with their family life."[23] It is fascinating that most young adults, including those who live at home to save money for college as well as those who live a distance away, tend to be "most satisfied" with family life.

Barna's research also points to 18-to-24-year-olds as being most guilty of leaving local communities of faith. This points to the higher importance of parents taking the lead in the spiritual development of teenagers.[24] Those in their late adolescent years (their mid-twenties) are in just as much need of parental involvement as junior high students. This should remain on the hearts of youth pastors across the nation who are often taking on more responsibility for ministry among those in this age group.

PARENTS NEED HELP

When their children are young, parents tend to recognize their responsibility for the spiritual growth of their children. One study by Barna Research Group reported that 85 percent of the parents of children under age 13 believe they have primary responsibility for teaching their children about religious beliefs and spiritual matters.[25] This is very encouraging; but as these children move into their teenage years, something else happens.

Many parents of teenagers generally rely upon the church to provide all the religious training their youth will receive. It's not so much that parents are unwilling to provide more substantive training to their teenage children. It's that they feel ill-equipped to do such work. According to Barna's research, parents typically have not planned for the spiritual development of their teenagers. They do not consider it a priority, have little or no training in how to nurture a teenager's faith, have no related standards or goals that they are seeking to satisfy, and experience no accountability for their efforts.[26] These are exciting times for youth leaders to connect with parents.

Barna went on to speak about the need for churches to help parents take the lead in raising their teens spiritually. "Parents have their children for many hours each week and experience numerous opportunities to teach their kids vital principles in a range of settings and situations. The more intentional a church is about giving parents the confidence and the tools to raise up spiritual champions, the more effective we found the congregation's parents to be as spiritual mentors."[27] We who are passionate about the next generation becoming mature Jesus-following adults have an opportunity to come alongside parents to train them how to take on their God-given role as spiritual caregivers to their teenagers.

PARENTS WANT PARTNERSHIP

Okay, now it's confession time. I admit that early in my own ministry parents intimidated me. I thought: *How can I, a young twentysomething, possibly understand what the parent of a teenager is going through?* And the truth is, I really didn't know everything these parents were dealing with. But understanding God's design for the role of parents in the spiritual formation of teenagers, I knew it was my calling to partner with the parents of the young people I was working with. So with humility and a learning posture, I learned to see parents in a different light and to engage them in the ministry.

Our mindset needs to shift from tolerating the parents of the teenagers in our ministries to partnering with those parents. For some youth pastors, this will require time alone with God and confession. For others, it simply means a reorganization of priorities and a change in our approach.

In *Think Orange,* Reggie Joiner's bright orange book for leaders of the next generation of children and teenagers, Joiner shares four levels of possible parental involvement in the spiritual growth of their teenage children. Youth workers seeking to partner with parents need to understand and support parents at each of these levels.[28] First, there are parents who are Aware of and concerned about specific situations in their child's life. These parents are often outside the church, but they still have a level of interest in becoming a better parent. Second, there are those who are Involved, at least at some level, in their teen's spiritual growth. These parents have a foot in the door of the church—bringing their teenagers to youth group and worship and recognizing that they influence their children spiritually. Third, there are parents who are Engaged and committed to partnering with the church. They are growing in their own relationship with God and assume the responsibility of being spiritual leaders in the home. The final and deepest level of parental connection features parents who are Invested in the spiritual development of their teenage children. They are devoting time and energy in partnership with the church. They understand the strategy of your ministry and are connected to other parents of teenagers in the congregation.

LEVELS OF PARTNERSHIP WITH PARENTS

These are how parents are involved in their teenagers' spiritual development and church.

1. AWARE
2. INVOLVED
3. ENGAGED
4. INVESTED

We need to seek ways to partner with and support parents who are at each of these levels. Your youth ministry calendar is probably already packed with good programs and events. The key is to brainstorm opportunities to partner with parents in the midst of what we are already doing. Here are just a few ways you might do that:

1. Use retreats to bring on a team of parents to plan and even be the speaking team or panel for those teenagers participating. Have parents share their struggles and successes in life. They can share their stories of coming to know Jesus as Savior and how they are making him Lord of their lives today.

2. Use small groups to help parents better understand what teenagers are experiencing. Invite a parent of every teenager in the group to come to their small group. This might seem weird to some teens at first, but over time this could become a rite of passage for parents.

3. Use mission trips to your advantage by partnering with parents. Plan and lead short-term trips combining parents and teenagers. Make it a family mission trip.

4. Consider involving parents in Bible studies with youth. Parents could serve as leaders or hosts, or they might just participate in the group alongside their kids. Rotate the homes where teenagers meet, providing more contact with parents.

5. Seek local service opportunities where youth and parents can get their hands dirty together. This is a great way to connect families in a nonthreatening way. Many churches already have partnerships with mission and service organizations. Use these connections to help parents serve in the name of Jesus alongside their teenagers.

6. If your church offers Sunday school classes for all ages, why not offer a "parenting teenagers" class or a "parents and teens together" class? You can start by offering a class that's just three or four weeks long, which is long enough to evaluate how it's going. A class with parents and teens together can provide a great opportunity for families to discuss issues without parents feeling like they have to "force" such conversations on their kids. It helps when someone else is the facilitator!

7. Finally, summer camps are a great way to help families come together. Many denominations and parachurch groups offer opportunities for parents and teenagers (as well as children) to gather in a family camp environment.

Most ministries already provide many of these kinds of activities for the youth involved. With an intergenerational mindset that emphasizes helping families connect, take another look at the calendar of events in your youth ministry. How can you create more opportunities to partner with parents?

Where will our country find leaders with integrity, courage, strength—all the family values—in ten, twenty, or thirty years? The answer is that parents are teaching them, loving them, and raising them right now.

—Unknown Author

DISCIPLESHIP, DEVELOPMENT, AND PARENTING

We'll be discussing discipleship later in the book; but in the context of this chapter, it is important to say just a little bit about the unique role of parents in discipling their teenage children. As you'll see in that chapter, I think of the discipleship process in three stages: Selection, Association, and Instruction. When it comes to parents, the first two steps of the process are already done! God has already selected parents to play a key role in the lives of their teenage children, and has provided the close association that makes true discipleship possible. The place where youth workers and other church leaders can help parents is in the third stage: Instruction.

What should parents of adolescents instruct their children to be and do? There are many good resources in this area. Some might say all we need is the Bible, but I believe parents need an intentional and strategic plan for using the Bible—such as the one we'll talk about more in the chapter on discipleship. I also believe it's important to remind parents that discipleship is more of a dance or art form; it's not a science with a checklist of things to accomplish. First and foremost, if a parent is not passionate about pursuing maturity in his or her own relationship with the Father, Son, and Holy Spirit, then the teenage son or daughter is going to have a hard time trusting anything the parent says about discipleship. But if both parent and teenager are willing to dedicate their lives to knowing Jesus and making him known, then the opportunities for families to grow together in Christ are numerous.

Another area where youth workers can provide significant support to parents concerns the realities of adolescent development. The Search Institute's list of 40 Developmental Assets for Internal and External Impact (presented in the last chapter) can be a tremendous resource to share as we come alongside parents in partnership. If parents—those who have the greatest spiritual impact and biblical responsibility for their teenagers—would do their best to support the growth of these assets in their children, the likelihood that they will become healthy and mature Jesus-following adults is very good. Youth workers have a strategic opportunity to share with parents of teenagers—

one on one, in small support groups, or during large group training times—the importance of these values for developmental maturity.

Can you imagine what a gift your sharing this list might be to a struggling or teachable parent? Many parents of teenagers are looking for categories and benchmarks of success. They are somewhat lost and at a crossroads of confusion as they seek to raise their teenagers into spiritual giants for God. This list of external and internal assets could bring fresh air to parents and build your relationship with them for more strategic partnership.

ADD UP THE ENVIRONMENTS

Most of the adolescents we work with have three main environments: Home, school, and church. It's hard to underestimate the importance of having caring adults surrounding our youth in each of these environments.

The power of providing caring connections with adults in each of these environments was made clear in a massive study of 12,000 teenagers in grades six to twelve.[29] The study looked at 38 items that served to measure the adolescents' maturity of faith, and it also allowed youth to describe their home, school, and church environments. The results showed strong connections between faith development and each of these environments. It should be no surprise that when home, school, and church environments are all positive, safe, and caring, adolescents are quite likely to develop and mature in their faith. But when just one or two of these environments is nurturing, the likelihood of a teen developing a mature faith decreases drastically.

As Christian leaders who care deeply about the next generation, it should be our desire to help all three of these locations flourish with health. Unfortunately, many youth workers focus almost entirely on just one of these places of influence—the church. A new mindset for intergenerational ministry demands that we have an influence on all three environments.

Yes, the role we play in helping to provide a caring church environment for adolescents within our congregation and youth ministries is critical. But we must also partner with parents to affect the home and get to know teachers and administrators who can get our feet in the door of the schools. We need a new mindset that stresses the importance of partnering with parents and educators in intergenerational ministry.

A new day has dawned. We can't continue to operate out on "Youth Ministry Island," disconnected from the moms and dads who have the greatest influence over and responsibility for the teens in our ministries. We need a new vision for ministry that emphasizes partnership with parents of teenagers.

Acting is just a way of making a living; the family is life.

—Denzel Washington

Throughout my years in ministry, I have found many parents who really want to understand and nurture the faith of their teenage son or daughter, but they need a plan. Recently, I led a three-week seminar on parenting teenagers where I shared many of the concepts in this book. More than 80 parents showed up for the seminar—and we had to move from a classroom to the gym. I'm convinced the interest and hunger is high for many parents. Share the information in this book and help them plan ways to be involved.

Remember, parents, not youth workers, have the greatest opportunity to shape the faith of the next generation. It is our God-given responsibility to get the vision for partnership and share it with others. Parents are looking for ways to engage. With a change of thinking and a new mindset for ministry, partnership with parents will become fun and fruit-filled.

CONTINUE THE CONVERSATION

1. Were you surprised by any of the research in this chapter? What surprised you most?
2. What has been your observation of the state of families today?
3. Knowing that parents still have the greatest spiritual influence on students, how do we come alongside them with training and tools?
4. How will you be a cheerleader for parents in your ministry?
5. How could you help parents become more invested in your ministry and the local church?

4
SWIMMING UPSTREAM
RIDING THE WAVES OF A CHANGING CULTURE

Without culture, Christianity is an abstraction unrelated to human life.

—Robert Pazmino

An understanding of culture is basic to Christian youth work . . . Christian youth workers must be culturally bilingual.

—Peter Ward

It's become clearer and clearer to me that if families just let the culture happen to them, they end up fat, addicted, broke, with a house full of junk and no time.

—Mary Pipher

When we pay attention to the cultural landscape, when we take time to explore the individual tiles of the mosaic, we will have a much better sense of the complete human picture.

—Duffy Robbins

Youth culture is everything that adolescents are exposed to and participate in that has to do with their friends, society, media, school and family.

—Dan Lambert

For years my family headed south to Florida during spring break—like so many other residents of Michigan, Indiana, and Ohio. During the winter months, there was a mass exodus from the northern states to the Gulf of Mexico. I am surprised Florida didn't sink into the sea each spring break.

I'll never forget one spring break when I was in elementary school. Many members of our family were enjoying a gorgeous day at the beach. I went for a swim in the Gulf, and I decided to head out a little further than I should have. I soon found myself being sucked out by the tide. I was a small kid and didn't have much fat to keep me afloat. It quickly became evident to me that I needed help. So I yelled for my dad who was sitting on the beach. He came running down and swam out to get me. After what seemed like days, I was rescued and safe.

Our contemporary culture is dragging many adolescents out to sea. There are a host of negative influences that threaten to drown our identities in Christ, the church's biblical mission, and healthy families and communities. Kids need help to avoid being pulled under by these dangerous waters.

The first step in responding is to call on our heavenly Father for guidance and help. If you do not already have a group of adults who gather and pray regularly for your ministry to youth, start one today. Put this book down right now, get on the phone, and set up a prayer time for tomorrow. Really. We need to understand the culture around us and strategically customize intergenerational ministry in order to make a kingdom difference in this world. But that process has to be grounded in prayer for our kids and our ministry.

As somebody who is going into youth ministry, I think it is crucial that the youth in our churches get connected with the older generations. I think the youth have a lot to learn from older people in the church.

—Mitchell, Youth Ministry Student

CHALLENGING WATERS

The word *culture* refers to a way of living that has become normative for a group of human beings. It includes, but is not limited to, music, art, media, and other thought patterns that influence norms or values. We shape and are shaped by the culture around us—and that influence can be positive or negative. Cultural forces can strengthen our best values and bring us closer to Christ, or culture can suck us out to sea.

Within any given culture, there are also many different subcultures. Our kids are swimming through the waters of numerous subcultures each day. Youth culture, church culture, school culture, Internet culture, and family culture are just a few of the subcultures that we youth workers should be considering.

The mass media has a huge role in shaping contemporary culture. Today, many media encourage a "me" mentality, especially in the United States. Self-gratification, individualism, anti-authoritarianism, and more can shape the attitudes of adolescents, families, and communities—even the local church in all of her forms. And the mass media is especially influential in shaping the hearts and minds of our young people.

In their influential 1985 book *Habits of the Heart*, Dr. Robert Bellah and his colleagues published their research on how media is shaping American culture.[1] Many of their findings are even truer today than they were 25 years ago. Bellah wrote about the dominant influence of individualism in American culture. This is especially true in the teenage subculture. He expressed his findings: "The meaning of one's life for most Americans is to become one's own person, almost to the point of giving birth to oneself."[2] This self-focus moves far beyond the healthy process of adolescents seeking individuation as part of their proper development toward becoming mature adults. What Bellah describes is a narcissistic and destructive pursuit that makes it difficult for individuals to commit themselves to their marriages, families, church congregations, jobs, or other organizations.

I find this analysis fascinating in a day when many young adults (late adolescent twentysomethings) like both big events (concerts, large worship gatherings) and smaller communal gatherings (small groups, some house churches, coffee-shop meetings), but many do not want to commit to a local body of believers. They will "commit" to Facebook, email lists, Podcasts, online subscriptions, gym memberships, and blogs for a time on their own terms; but by and large, most are reluctant to commit to an intergenerational local body of believers. Do you know why? The "me-first" culture has tempted the next generation into thinking that submission to authority (including God), humility, and commitment are antiquated values, not present biblical realities. And the cultural undertow is pulling our young people out into dangerous waters.

Youth culture is influenced by the culture-shaping power of mass consumerism. That drives a lot of educational imperatives, career aspirations, family decisions, even views of romance. Life is about succeeding in a career to get money to spend to have fun. People are essentially consumers. Society is redefined as a big market. Religious faith is, at best, a consumer commodity to enjoy or not. Technological and media influences are part of this but secondary.

—Christian Smith, *The Youthworker Journal Roundtable on Kids and Youth Culture*

THE CHANGING LANDSCAPE

Youth workers, parents, and other caring adults do not need to go to Bible college or seminary to know that the culture is changing. We are all living in it and are aware of the shift, intuitively if not consciously. We feel the tide as it shifts directions. Think about these societal changes of the past five decades that deeply affect adolescent lives:

- **Technology is shifting faster than light speed.** It is amazing to think that a digital wristwatch has more computer power than what existed in the whole world before 1961.[3] (And most kids today don't even wear these watches— they just check the time on their cell phones!) "Online" used to describe the birds on the telephone wires outside your house. I remember the bookshelf full of encyclopedias that my parents had downstairs, and I used them for research papers in high school. Now information in the world's libraries is at your finger-tips. Google handles about 1 billion search queries a day.[4] Did you catch that? Yes, *1 billion* a day.

    One week, as I was teaching our church college group on Sunday morning, I mentioned a fact I'd heard about some national monument, and a twentysome-thing corrected me. She'd used her iPhone to do a Google search and found that what I'd said was wrong. We now live in a world of instant correction. And George Barna's research has shown that an increasing number of teams now use the Internet for "finding spiritual or religious experiences."[5] Computer technol-ogy gives teenagers access to both good and bad spiritual influences with the touch of a key. This is why youth workers need to help teens develop a biblical worldview that helps them be discerning.

    Consider more technological advances. There are more than 1 billion com-puters in use around the world. More than 160 billion emails are sent daily. (It is interesting that 97 percent of that email is considered spam.) There are 2 billion televisions in use as you read this, and more than 4 billion cell phones in use. The first public cell phone call was made on April 3, 1973, by Martin Cooper. Consumers around the world will purchase around 3 million cell phones . . . *today*. About 10 hours worth of video viewing is uploaded every minute on YouTube. On average, United States users view 100 videos a month. Flickr hosts some 3 billion photographs, while Facebook hosts more than 10 billion.[6] New technologies are reshaping modern life, and our young people are at the center of those changes.

- *Sex* **is an everyday word—in the media, as well as on the lips (and in the text messages) of our teenagers.** In the three decades since the intro-duction of the birth control pill, premarital and extramarital sexual behavior are now seen as the norm in Western culture. As I write this book, revelations about world-renowned professional golfer Tiger Woods' multiple extramarital affairs are hitting the news. Ten or twenty years ago, this news might have been shocking, but today it seems par for the course. How unfortunate when our society's "positive role model" celebrities cheat on their spouses (and deeply affect their children). Kids are surrounded by media messages that tell them any and all forms of sexual expression and experimentation are normal. Kids download pornographic pictures from the Internet and send them to others on their cell phones. There's plenty of cultural pressure encouraging adolescents to disregard God's instructions about sexual behavior.

- **As our culture grows more and more diverse, cultural relativism becomes more and more common.** Multiculturalism is a beautiful display of God's creativity. We can celebrate our nation's growing diversity and the fact that our children are taught to value the richness of the world's people and cultures like never before. The problem comes when this appreciation of cultural differences translates into a belief that all truth is relative and every kind of belief and behavior is equally acceptable because it's "all good." There is a subliminal message that encourages kids to mix and match their own belief systems—take a little from here and a little from there, throw it all in a blender, and mix up your own spiritual smoothie to drink. Teaching and training adolescents to be "sharp" with a belief system centered on the Father, Son, and Holy Spirit is the key to maintaining a mature Christian faith amidst these competing values.

- **The local church no longer holds all the cards on faith.** In the late 1800s and early 1900s, the local church was at the center of Christian life. Today, even many who call themselves Christian have adopted a "do-it-yourself" approach to the faith that's away from the life of the local body of believers. Now you can "do church" sitting in front of your computer (or maybe this is not church at all). This has huge implications for the way the next generation of youth and young adults view church leadership authority, spiritual growth, church government, and church discipline. The claims of the local church are now up for grabs because of societal and technological influences.

- **People are working longer hours and spending less time at home, increasing the strain on families.** Economic pressures and the disease of "workaholism" are causing parents to spend more time at their jobs. This affects the amount of time families have with one another, the modeling of biblical values in the home, and what adolescents see as the norm for adulthood. Some parents value money and materialism over quality and quantity time with their children. With the work-related absence of some moms and dads from the lives of their teenagers, the pressure to grow up fast is clear.

As we look across the cultural horizon, the pace of change is overwhelming. Trees and farmhouses have been replaced with high-rise buildings and suburbs full of fenced-in homes. Libraries and bookstores are giving way to online resources, information, and purchases. Face-to-face community encounters are being replaced by cell phone texting and online social community Web sites. Times are changing fast. By the time this book is in print, I am sure some of the illustrations and statistics will already be out of date. Youth workers need to make adjustments intentionally and strategically if we want to avoid being taken out to sea.

One weekday edition of the *New York Times* includes more information than the average person encountered in his entire lifetime in 17th century England. The average consumer will see or hear one million marketing messages in a year. That's almost 3,000 per day.

—Leonard Sweet, *Soul Tsunami*

GROWING UP TOO FAST

Brace yourself for a difficult question: If kids are being forced to grow up too fast in our culture, who is rushing them?

There are many different contributors—but I believe the pressure often begins in the home. Parents are under great strain today in our fast-paced, pressure-packed world—and in many cases, this causes the "wheels to fall off the wagon." Divorce, long work hours, self-centeredness, and fear of the future are realities of the parental world. Parents may seek to escape these realities by living through their children, especially as it relates to academic and athletic success. David Elkind has suggested that some parents compensate for disinterest in their own jobs by becoming very involved in their children's athletic "careers." Elkind writes, "I would venture that there is a strong tie between job dissatisfaction, on the one hand, and disproportionate concern with offspring's success in sports, on the other. Children thus became the symbols or carriers of their parents' frustrated competitiveness in the workplace. The parent can take pride in the child's success or blame the coach for his or her failure."[7] (This can be really difficult if that parent is also the child's coach!) The pressure that many young people feel coming from parents on the sidelines of school and athletic events can lead to unhealthy identity development.

As a parent I have seen all this—the "my" church within the church, the "me-focused" theology, and the attitude that says "new" is always better and more exciting than the "old"! I try to stay connected and a supporter of my home church, my children's schools, the youth groups, Bible studies, and more! Every parent needs to be more proactive about encouraging the youth and those working with them! Prayer is vital! Words of love and encouragement are vital! A hug is vital! One leader cannot do it all, one church can't do it all! We must go to the Father for wisdom, guidance, and his Holy Spirit empowerment!

—Anonymous, Parent of a Teenager

Additionally, schools often succumb to the worldly pressures that encourage students to grow up too fast. Our culture has put more expectations, more hours, more homework, more testing, and more requirements on students than any other time in history. Overcrowded schools are forced to follow a cookie-cutter model for all children and teenagers, ignoring individual differences in mental abilities, learning rates, and learning styles of students. The pressure teachers and school administrators feel to "hurry" students along is not their fault. I love teachers, and I know they are doing the best job they can amid a system that's been put in place to push students through the assembly line of learning. Teachers have a difficult job in a difficult and stress-filled environment.

Certainly, the media also play a large part in encouraging adolescents to grow up very fast. Movies, magazines, the Internet, and television have all sped up the treadmill of growing up. Interestingly, these increasingly visual forms of entertainment stimulate all the senses . . . *fast*. They don't engage our thinking in the same way a good book or an old radio program does. Marshall McLuhan, Canadian media analyst, suggests that these visual types of media extend our senses and do not always require any kind of verbal commentary—the images speak for themselves.[8] It's no wonder developing adolescents identify with and want to be like the characters they watch in visual media—whether they are real-life celebrities or fictional characters.

Recently, 19-year-old country music superstar Taylor Swift won the "Performer of the Year" award during the 2009 Country Music Awards (CMAs) live television show. Having a teenager win the biggest honor in country music doesn't help her, nor does it help all the other teenagers who watched her win the award. These adolescents begin to think it's normal to be hurried into adulthood, taking center stage with lots of money and prestige in front of the whole world.

The recent hit movie series based on the *Twilight* books connects with adolescents at multiple levels. The four books in the series were among the top-selling books on the *USA Today* list in 2009. I had the opportunity to watch the first *Twilight* movie on the long plane flight to Africa for a mission trip. Weeks later, I mentioned the movie while speaking at a youth camp. The chatter among the 100 teenagers in the room began to build. I talked about the unrealistic expectations about romance and sensual relationships that were being communicated (or sold) to them through the movie. Any girl who expects the "man of her dreams" to be able to carry her on his back, run up trees, and play piano while serenading her with his beautiful voice (they started giggling) is sure to be disappointed (they stopped giggling). Our youth look to media for reality, but we need to teach them discernment as they seek God's wisdom. This is an essential but difficult task for youth workers.

I've tried to paint a quick picture of the cultural pressure that surrounds and hurries our youth today. I believe that most youth workers, parents, and other adults recognize intuitively that it's a stressful time for adolescents. Add this cultural pressure to their feelings of loneliness and abandonment, and we have a hurricane on our shores that must be calmed.

FACING CULTURE HEAD ON

So what kind of relationship should Christians have with the surrounding culture? Over time, different Christians have answered this question in different ways. Personally, I believe we can change culture for good—not completely, but at least some. As we head toward Jesus' second return and the full revelation of his glorious kingdom, we strive today toward shaping ourselves and our world for the glory of God.

In his classic book *Christ and Culture*, H. Richard Niebuhr described five different ways Christians can relate to culture:

Christ of Culture	Christ Above Culture	Christ the Transformer of Culture	Christ and Culture in Paradox	Christ Against Culture
Cultural Christians	Synthesists	Conversionalists	Dualists	Separatist Christians
"Jesus is the Great Teacher and Role Model."				"Light has no fellowship with darkness."

The Christ Against Culture view sees contemporary culture as completely opposed to Christianity. Those in this belief category believe Christians must separate themselves from a modern society dominated by sin and "the flesh." (See 1 John 2:16 and 2 Corinthians 6:17.) Many very conservative and fundamentalist Christians fall in this category. The Amish community is one extreme example in which many rules and regulations are stressed to keep clear of the "evil world." While I believe such rigid boundaries can effectively reduce the temptation to sin, the risk in such a view is that we may lose track of grace. If there is no grace, the gospel is not present.

One the other end of the scale is the Christ of Culture. Here's how Niebuhr describes these believers: "There are those who feel no great tension between the church and the world, the social norms and the gospel, the workings of divine grace and human effort, the ethics of salvation and the ethics of social progress."[9] For these folks, being a good Christian and being a good cultural citizen are very similar. Many youth workers and pastors of all types reflect this in their planning and philosophy of ministry. Social gatherings, fun activities, and keeping everyone (both youth and parents) happy and smiling are the goals of ministry. Being good in one's behavior equals being a good Christian. The danger for this group is that faith gets reduced to the all-inclusive idea of just being a "good person." When grace is used as a license to sin and the holiness of God is not preached, foolish living follows.

Between these two poles, are three other attitudes Christians might take toward culture. Niebuhr suggests that the majority of Christians fall into the Christ Above Culture area on the scale. These Christians find a middle ground between the extremes of all grace and no grace. Because God created the world and Jesus interacted with it in spirit and nature, they believe we cannot be in opposition to culture. Niebuhr writes that this view sees Christ not as against culture, but as using culture's "best products as instruments in his work of bestowing on men what they cannot achieve by their own efforts."[10]

A fourth way of understanding Christ's relationship with culture is called Christ and Culture in Paradox. According to Niebuhr, this is a "both-and" position that calls for "dualism." Like the "Christ Against Culture" group, these Christians see the world as very sick and godless. But they know they have been placed in this fallen world and are a part of it, so they look to God to sustain and protect them within it. The Paradox group does not see the world as "completely evil" because they have been regenerated through salvation. Dualists are not focused on changing culture, just seeking to live out their faith until Jesus returns.

Finally, the fifth group (in the very middle of the chart) sees Christ as the Transformer of Culture. These Christians believe culture is fully under God's sovereign control and grace. As a result, they engage culture as a work of obedience to God's calling. Theirs is a balanced approach to being "in the world, but not of the world." This group believes that living out the Christian life, while it may sometimes involve separating ourselves from some elements of culture, more often involves full engagement in improving social conditions for the glory of God.

Niebuhr points out that there are strengths and weaknesses to each of these five ways of living in culture as a Christian. Rather than stating definitively that there is any "one way" for believers to relate to the surrounding culture, he shows the ways faithful Christians have lived out each of these responses.

I believe Niebuhr's book is very helpful for church leaders as we wrestle with how we are to engage with culture and minister to the next generation. As youth workers, we need to help adolescents develop a strong theology that shapes how they will live in this world. Personally, I think the most biblically faithful response is found near the center of Niebuhr's scale, rather than on one pole or the other. Open and honest discussion among mature believers is critical if we are going to reach and disciple the next generation for God's glory.

Good theology needs three kinds of exegesis or efforts at interpretation. Followers of Jesus, in our complex and rapidly changing culture, must exegete or interpret (1) themselves, (2) their culture, and (3) the Scriptures. Know yourself, understand what is happening in society, and ... study the Word of God.

—Dean Borgman, *This Way to Youth Ministry*

HOW DO YOU VIEW THE WORLD?

Years ago, my son got a book called *1001 Pirate Things to Spot*. Like the *Where's Waldo?* books where Waldo can be found hiding on every page, this book tests your observational skills—but in this case, you're searching for pirates, parrots, cannons, swords, flags, anchors, boats, and treasure. It was so much fun sitting with Levi and looking for pirates and the "treasures" hidden on each page. "There's one!" he would say each time we found one. The funny thing was, the longer we looked at each picture, the easier it was to see the pirates. Over time, you learn where to look and where not to look. It's as if your eyes get a new focus that helps you see what you couldn't see earlier.

The same is true about finding God's truth in this world. The longer you look at the real Father, Son, and Holy Spirit that is revealed in the Scriptures (and not some counterfeit cultural image), the easier it is to see God in the world. When your view of God is clear, you're able to focus on him in the attitudes and actions of people. Making this distinction between the real and fake God is called discernment.

As youth workers walk alongside adolescents, we need to help them get a focused biblical view of the world. There is no question that the world is full of hurt, destruction, greed, jealousy, and pride. The best defense we can offer young people is a theology that helps them know what they believe and why they believe it. Such a worldview will form their Identity, Autonomy, and Belonging. It will help them mature well. Classrooms and cubicles are full of counterfeits. Those who care for the next generation must help them develop eyes that can see God's truth.

Every adolescent you work with is forming his or her own worldview—and those views are heavily influenced by culture whether teens realize it or not. I don't need to tell you that adolescents encounter a wide range of perspectives in the classrooms, workplaces, malls, grocery stores, and coffee shops in their world—just listen to the way teenagers, friends, coworkers, and others talk about the way they see the world and make decisions.

The questions Niebuhr considers in those five descriptions of Christ and Culture are key for those of us who minister with youth. How do we view the world? Is this world a sinful place to be avoided? Should we embrace this world as a reflection of the God who created it and everything in it? Or are we to find some middle ground where we live in this world in a way that can transform it for God's glory?

Oh, the depth of the riches of the wisdom and knowledge of God! How unsearchable his judgments, and his paths beyond tracing out! "Who has known the mind of the Lord? Or who has been his counselor?" "Who has ever given to God, that God should repay him?" For from him and through him and to him are all things. To him be the glory forever! Amen.

—Paul in Romans 11:33–36

So what is *your* worldview? Sometimes even youth workers mix up their understandings of the world. In the name of liking Jesus or spirituality, but not liking the organized church or religion, we blur the lines of genuine orthodox Christian belief. We need to be very careful not to create a counterfeit god in our own image, but to maintain a biblical worldview as we lead adolescents to Christ. We are the created ones; God is the Creator. Be discerning as you plan, think, and pray about intergenerational ministry. Ask strategic questions to help your youth get to the bottom of their own worldviews, and lead them to Jesus Christ and his truth as they journey toward becoming spiritually mature adults.

BEAUTIFULLY TURBULENT WATERS

Whitewater rafting is a rush. The freezing water that splashes in your face as the raft drops several feet straight down is exhilarating. Every time I sign up to take a group of kids rafting, I dread it at first; but once we're out on the river, I love it. At times it seems out of control, full of close calls; but in the end, our guide directs our path. It is a beautiful adventure.

The same can be said of helping adolescents navigate the contemporary culture that surrounds them. Youth ministry is a cross-cultural endeavor. Understanding what is happening in our world and in our church can help us connect more effectively with teenagers. Duffy Robbins puts it this way: "Understanding youth culture can help us reflect on how to be culturally relevant without being biblically relativistic."[11]

The teenage world may seem miles away from the adult world, and the gulf between them might be getting wider as time passes. But as adults who care deeply about adolescents, we must dig in deeper and do the hard work of an anthropologist. We must know the kids we are trying to reach and the culture in which they live. Youth workers today have the challenge of being missionaries to a generation in desperate need of love, acceptance, and care. This is a beautiful pursuit.

CONTINUE THE CONVERSATION

1. How do you think culture is influencing adolescents today?
2. Which of the "changing landscape" factors do you think is the most challenging for youth ministry?
3. How have you seen adolescents being hurried to grow up too fast today?
4. What is your strategy for teaching your students about a Christian worldview?
5. How does your ministry context address and engage with "Christ and Culture"?

5
BEING THE POINT PERSON

THOUGHTFUL REFLECTIONS ON LEADERSHIP

There is no more powerful engine driving an organization toward excellence and long-range success than an attractive, worthwhile, achievable vision of the future, widely shared.

—Burt Nanus

All good leaders are good learners, and the moment you stop learning you stop leading.

—Rick Warren

Advancement in the kingdom is not by climbing but by kneeling. Since the Lord has become Servant of all, any special calling in his name must be a calling to humility, to service. The stairway to the ministry is not a grand staircase but a back stairwell that leads to the servants' quarters.

—Edmund P. Clowney

We heard people say, "Everyone is called." But in the Scriptures, God specifically calls some to shepherd His people. The call and the enabling are special. Do not let anyone explain away your high calling, and make it common to all. It is not common!"

—Henry Blackaby, Henry Brandt, and Kerry L. Skinner

I will take the Ring, though I do not know the way.

—Frodo Baggins, in J. R. R. Tolkien's *The Lord of the Rings*

Leadership is a strange thing. As leaders, we are asked to take responsibility for a particular set of people, but true leadership can't be forced or manipulated. Leadership in youth ministry is even more challenging because leaders must interact with students, parents, and volunteers. Within all these relationships there is a particular dance of accountability that occurs.

Complicating things is the fact that most youth workers are not at the very top of the leadership pyramid. Most youth ministers are in what's often called a "middle-leadership" or "second-chair" position.[1] Depending on the structure of your church or organization, you may be accountable to the senior pastor, a board of elders or deacons, or another supervisor. Providing leadership within your ministry while also submitting to the direction of your supervisors can be a delicate dance indeed! You may feel squished like the cream inside an Oreo cookie! But when the recipe is right, it can taste so good.

When it comes to Christian leadership, Jesus set the example for us. Jesus' model for leadership is contrary to the world's model in many ways. The world and its systems are dominated by prideful leaders who selfishly climb to the top in any way possible. James and John reflected this worldly understanding when they asked Jesus if they could sit on his right and left when Jesus came into his kingdom. They sought power and control by climbing higher up the chain of command. But Jesus taught them that his kind of leadership demands becoming a servant of all (Mark 10:35–45). And he gave his disciples an object lesson in Christian leadership, just hours before he went to the cross, when he washed their feet (John 13). Jesus was the greatest leader of all not because of his power and control (although he had it at his fingertips), but because of his tender, compassionate, and submissive heart. He was a servant of all. This is the kind of leadership to which we are called.

Whether you've just landed your first job at a local church or you've been serving in the same church or ministry for decades, leadership is part of your job as a youth worker. To be in ministry requires leadership, but *servant leadership*. Even if you are a parent or volunteer serving in youth ministry, leadership is a bridge that must be crossed.

Christian leadership requires that we die to ourselves to serve our calling. I like what A. W. Tozer says about the motivations for Christian leadership: "A true and safe leader is likely to be one who has no desire to lead, but is forced into a position of leadership by the inward pressure of the Holy Spirit and the press of the external situation."[2] In other words, the good and right leader for the next generation is one who is very cautious to lead in the first place. This is humility. Taking responsibility as a Christian leader should never be done in isolation or purely of our own desire. Christian leadership is a response to God's calling, and should be affirmed by the family of God.

HEADING INTO LEADERSHIP

As we put on a new mindset for intergenerational ministry, we need to think carefully about what it means to be in a ministry leadership position. In John Maxwell's wonderful book *Developing the Leader Within You*, he invites readers to reflect on what he calls the five levels of leadership.[3] Each of the levels offers a different answer to the question, "Why do people follow you?"

Think about the youth in your ministry, as well as the adult volunteers, parents, and others with whom you work. What motivates them to follow your leadership? How do they perceive you? Why would they follow you as their leader? Maxwell suggests five possible reasons.

1. **Position (Rights).** Some people might be following you simply because of your position, or title as youth pastor, youth director, or volunteer leader. They follow you because of your "rights" as a leader. The ministry says you have the leadership role, and some will follow you for that reason alone. But if that's the only reason, then your influence will never extend beyond the tasks in your job description. The longer you stay in the position you are in, the higher the turnover and the lower the morale of those who are following you. People will begin to limit your influence and put "fences" around you. You will not be able to stay at this level for longer than two years, Maxwell says.

2. **Permission (Relationships).** Others will follow you because of your "relationship" with them. They follow because they've chosen to do so. They enjoy being connected to you and the ministry, so they give you permission to lead. This is good, but staying here too long will cause highly motivated followers to get restless.

3. **Production (Results).** Some people will follow you because they've seen your contribution to the organization. You have produced "results," and they like that. This is where most people sense your "success" in ministry. They like what you are doing, and so they follow your lead. At this level momentum is high and problems are fixed with little effort. But getting too comfortable at this level will cause the momentum to slow down.

4. **People Development (Reproduction).** Others will follow you because of what you have done for them personally. You are helping them develop as Christians, helping to "reproduce" Christ in them. Long-range growth occurs here. If you commit to invest your life in others, multiply leaders, an intergenerational ministry to youth will grow and expand. Getting to and staying at this level needs to be a priority.

5. **Personhood (Respect).** Hopefully, over time many will follow you because of who you are and what you represent. They follow your lead because they "respect"

you as a servant-leader. You have already come through the other levels, and your followers see it. This step is reserved for youth workers who have a long track record in growing people and ministries. Few make it to this level with faithfulness. Those who do have true humility.

Without exhausting all the definitions of leadership, possibly the most common one is summed up in the word *influence*. Leadership involves influencing the direction of others. One author defines leadership this way: "A leader takes people where they would never go on their own."[4] Youth workers are leading students in a direction that brings God the glory. But if the adolescents we work with aren't going anywhere, then we aren't leading. As John Maxwell has written, "He who thinks he is leading and has no one following him is only taking a walk."

Bringing individuals or groups in a certain direction is leadership. This direction and destination may be hazy or clear. The progress may be slow or fast. But leadership is a journey to somewhere. When Jesus looked out on the crowds in need of a leader, he viewed them as "harassed and helpless, like sheep without a shepherd" (Matthew 9:35–38). Youth workers of today are the shepherds called to lead, to take the next generation in a certain and clear direction. This is a great adventure and a privileged pilgrimage.

Leadership must be pursued downward. To be great, we must be last. For youth workers, this can be a battle for the heart. Do everything you can to make attitude everything as you lead.

JOHN MAXWELL'S LEVELS OF LEADERSHIP
WHY STUDENTS AND VOLUNTEERS FOLLOW YOU

- Position—"Rights"
- Permission—"Relationships"
- Production—"Results"
- People Development—"Reproduction"
- Personhood—"Respect"

While a select few may be born with a great deal of natural leadership abilities, for the most part leadership is learned. So no matter where you are on the growth curve of leadership, there is more to learn and enjoy. Be a sponge and soak up as much as you can from those around you—and then share what you've learned with others. George Bernard Shaw's words can easily be applied to leadership in youth ministry: "I want to be thoroughly used up when I die, for the harder I work, the more I live. I rejoice in life for its own sake. Life is no 'brief candle' to me. It is a sort of splendid torch which I have got a hold of for the moment, and I want to make it burn as brightly as possible before handing it on to future generations."[5]

Here are seven vital principles I have found to be good in leading an intergenerational ministry that will guide adolescents closer to Jesus. These principles are in no particular order, but each of them is essential to moving churches and ministries forward in faithful outreach to the next generation.

PRINCIPLE 1: BEGIN AT THE BOTTOM

Years ago, professional tennis player Andre Agassi was in a television ad for Canon cameras. After dipping tennis balls into different colored paint, he hit them against a wall and then took a photograph of his "artwork." The slogan of the advertisement was "Image is everything." What a picture of our culture today! (Pun intended.) Even Christian leaders seem to seek out spotlights and stages. This is a dangerous place to be.

The first vital leadership principle in an intergenerational mindset for ministry is "Begin at the Bottom." Image is *not* everything. Attitude is everything. Paul gave us great insight when he said, "Your attitude should be the same as that of Christ Jesus . . . [who] made himself nothing . . . he humbled himself and became obedient to death— even death on a cross." (Philippians 2:5–8, NIV). Christian leadership is grounded in humility and service to others.

The world is full of "top-down" leadership where the "lead dog" barks out orders saying, "I am in charge. You are not." This was not Jesus' model for us. His desire was for youth workers to go to the bottom fast by giving up their "rights" for the sake of the youth they serve.

When I first began working in youth ministry, I was full of zeal. I had the framed diploma on the wall of my office, lots of fresh ideas, bookshelves full of great ministry resources, and lots of energy and passion. I had the training, I had the job, and I thought I knew where the ministry needed to go. As a result, I did not submit well to the leaders above me. I thought I was always right (even when I didn't say so, which can be even worse!) I had to learn that joining the staff of a church or other ministry organization requires submission—first and foremost to the Lord, but also to the people God has placed in positions of supervision over you. I got this wrong at the beginning of my ministry, and I think it's a common mistake made by those in middle-leadership positions—even in the church. We have trouble submitting, but Peter appeals to us when he says, "Submit yourselves for the Lord's sake to every human authority . . ." (1 Peter 2:13). As leaders in youth ministry who focus on doing ministry together with the generations, we all need to continue learning to serve from a position of submission.

Even Jesus submitted to the Father's will all the way to the end of his earthly life (Luke 22:42).

Jesus was the master servant—and the way he lived provides a model for all who seek to lead. Just hours before he was betrayed and died on the cross for the sins of the world, he showed the disciples how to serve one another. John the Beloved wrote, "Jesus knew that the time had come for him to leave this world and go to the Father. Having loved his own who were in the world, he now showed them the full extent of his love" (John 13:1, NIV). John says that in that upper room Jesus showed the disciples the "full extent of his love." Really? How? He does so by taking the lowest position on the chain of command, the bond servant. He grabbed a towel, filled a basin with water, and began washing the disciples' feet in complete humility.

Remember that Jesus is fully God. He has the authority, position, and power to do whatever his heart desires. He could have demanded and dictated what the disciples would do. But instead he chose to lead by serving others.

This was Jesus' example to the disciples. This is what Jesus says we must do if we want to be real and true spiritual leaders. We must align our hearts and attitudes with Jesus'. The final explanation of Jesus' servant act comes later in the passage, when he says, "I have set you an example that you should do as I have done for you. Very truly I tell you, servants are not greater than their master, nor are messengers greater than the one who sent them. Now that you know these things, you will be blessed if you do them" (John 13:15–17). Note the connection between serving in humility and being blessed. Jesus emptied himself and became nothing. We who seek to follow in his way must "begin at the bottom"—whatever our role or title in the organization might be.

We youth workers have been given positions of authority, power, and control. But we are not leading in the spirit of Christ unless we approach our roles with humility. Here are some questions to contemplate: Are you looking to serve your volunteer leaders or are you demanding they serve you? Are you serving other church staff members or are you waiting for them to serve you? Are you encouraging and supporting the senior pastor and elders by serving them, or are you always complaining about what they do wrong? Do you see submitting to those in authority as a teachable gift or as a barrier that holds you back from greatness? Are you doing the little acts of service joyfully or for the praise of people? How you answer these questions would expose your heart and attitude toward servant-leadership. Spend some time with God and do some deep probing.

Leadership the way Jesus intended is not natural. It requires the unction of the Holy Spirit changing our minds and rearranging our hearts so they are aligned with the upside-down kingdom of God. To be a faithful leader, you must begin at the bottom.

PRINCIPLE 2: PUT PEOPLE FIRST

For many youth workers, this next principle is easy—or at least it *seems* easy. You love the youth you work with. The reason you landed this job at this place was because you wanted to spend time with teens and see them mature spiritually. You value your ministry volunteers and the parents involved in your ministry. If you're a youth worker, there's a pretty good chance you're a "people person." So why did I include "Put People First" as a key leadership principle?

Because the various responsibilities of ministry can often distract us from the very people we've been called to serve. As I've served in many local churches in youth and young adult positions, I have discovered that the more responsibility I have, the more office work there is to do. In addition, the more students and volunteer leaders you have and the larger your church or ministry is, the more tasks and planning are required. Many of us feel like we never have enough time to do all that's necessary. We have to make decisions about what we'll do, and what we'll leave undone. With so many competing demands, I have found I need to be very intentional about investing my life in people, and especially about making the effort to help connect the generations in meaningful relationships.

Putting people above tasks has not always felt natural for me. This may seem ironic because my primary calling as a minister of the gospel is to direct people toward God. But my natural God-given design gravitates toward tasks. These tasks that I do may be done with people in mind, but they are still tasks. Over the years this has gotten me in trouble, as I have not spent enough time with the right people. But over time I've found a better balance between people and paper—and you can, too.

The heart of leadership is influencing others toward God's purposes. Our goal is to see adolescents (and the entire church) grow to be holy. Paul explained it this way, "We proclaim him, admonishing and teaching everyone with all wisdom, so that we may present everyone fully mature in Christ. To this end I strenuously contend with all the energy Christ so powerfully works in me" (Colossians 1:28–29). This is our end product. We want to see teenagers and young adults mature to become more like Christ Jesus.

The people who have had the biggest impact in my life are those who shared biblical principles, modeled a godly life, and spent time with me. Leadership is influencing people, not accomplishing tasks. We need to learn to delegate tasks so we can spend more time with people—doing lunches with teenagers, taking time with our spouses and children, enjoying moments with ministry volunteers and parents, and walking around and connecting with others.

If someone interrupts you in the middle of some task (texting, emailing, "computering," writing, planning), stop and put the person first. These interruptions are not barriers to real ministry, but opportunities to love like Christ loved the church. Intergenerational ministry depends on a people focus.

PRINCIPLE 3: BUILD A TEAM

Every healthy intergenerational ministry is built with a team. Traditional youth ministries of the past often relied on hiring a youth pastor with a lively "personality" who would single-handedly keep the youth entertained and out of trouble. If this is your vision, you might not be in the right profession. Building and maintaining a faithful ministry takes seriously the responsibility of connecting the generations in healthy relationships—and that requires a team.

One of the most difficult roles any leader plays is that of team-builder. The role of the pastor is clearly written in Scripture. It is "to equip his people for works of service, so that the body of Christ may be built up" (Ephesians 4:12). Everything else you do in ministry—teaching lessons, building programs, planning events—is secondary. These other items are valuable, but they are not your first priority. Training and equipping volunteer leaders and parents is the best way to multiply God's ministry.

In his wonderful book for those heading into their first few years of youth ministry, Doug Fields provides a compelling list of reasons why teams in youth ministry are important.[6] I have adapted the list here. I believe all of these reasons fit well within an intergenerational mindset for ministry.

- Teams don't bottleneck growth. If you are ministering alone, your ministry will eventually stop growing and may even decrease numerically and spiritually. Jesus didn't minister directly to every single individual he encountered. He selected 12 people to hang with and equip for ministry, and he spent most of his time with just three guys. You cannot be everyone's "go-to" guy or gal. Connecting many older adults to the students in your care requires you to release and trust.
- Teams allow you to maintain more energy and will help you last longer in youth ministry. God does not want you to minister alone. He is all about relationships. As I have heard the stories from youth pastors in the trenches and have had my own early experiences, I've found that the most discouraged and fatigued youth pastors often struggle because they are trying to do it alone.
- Teams make your church stronger. Intergenerational ministry requires connection to the whole of the local church. You might be the most gifted communicator on the planet, a great "up-front" person, a fantastic game planner, and a student magnet, but you will never accomplish as much as God wants you to in ministry if you are trying to do it all. The body of Christ grows stronger as individuals are connected to one another across generational lines.
- Teams broaden the impact of your ministry. Many students will be attracted to you, but others will not. A strong team of volunteers and parents will help your

ministry reach different students. You do not need to become all things to all adolescents. You need a team.

- Teams help ministry skills increase. With an openness to learn, team members will learn from one another and help everyone get better. Even in areas where you feel strong, you may find teammates who are more polished in certain skills. Learn from them.
- Teams have more fun. It is hard to celebrate and throw a party alone. A team of intergenerational-minded workers can be the group you have the most fun with. Don't just pray and work together. Play together, too.

The leaders who work most effectively, it seems to me, never say "I." They don't *think* "I." They think "we"; they think "team." They understand their job to be to make the team function. They accept the responsibility and don't sidestep it, but "we" gets the credit. There is an identification (very often, quite unconscious) with the task and with the group. This is what creates trust, what enables you to get the task done.

—Peter Drucker, *Managing the Non-Profit Organization*

To take this list seriously, youth leaders need to view themselves as part of the team. Many youth pastors, especially those just starting out in ministry, view themselves as the center of the ministry. I challenge you to put young people in the center and surround them with a "constellation of adults."[7] In our youth ministry at Foothills Bible Church, we try to make sure at least five Jesus-following adults are involved in each teenager's life. There is a web of adults that surrounds each and every teen. This increases the likelihood that these young people will become mature Jesus-following adults when they transition out of adolescence and into adulthood. Within such a structure, your job as a leader is to recruit and train adults who can love, care for, and teach the adolescent for spiritual maturity in Christ.

As youth pastor, you have an important role—but every member of the team is important. And knowing you can't do it alone keeps you humble. Others on the team have jobs that are equally critical in helping youth grow in Christ. You play the role of a servant-leader by building your team to surround adolescents with adults. *Intergenerational ministry leaders do it together with a team!*

One facet of leadership is the ability to recognize the special abilities and limitations of others, combined with the capacity to fit each one into the job where he will do best.

—J. Oswald Sanders, *Spiritual Leadership*

PRINCIPLE 4: RECOGNIZE AND AFFIRM OTHERS

You may think I'm crazy or insecure, but for years I've had a file (the old-fashioned kind) where I keep notes of encouragement that I've received throughout the years. These are letters or emails that other leaders, congregation members, students, parents, and friends have sent to me. Every now and then, I get out the file, read over what they've written, and get some encouragement.

For years, organizational researchers have been saying that encouragement and affirmation are more effective motivators than financial incentives are, but many leaders still don't understand this. People love to be recognized for a job well done. Many of the "one another" commands in Scripture point to affirmation and love. The book of James talks about the power of the tongue, which can offer great affirmation or cause deep and long-lasting damage to the soul. Consider the many dysfunctional adults who struggle because they didn't receive much love and affirmation as children.

Ministry leaders should be quick to offer frequent affirmation of youth, volunteers, parents, senior pastors, coworkers, and all others within our spheres of influence. Part of our task of equipping the people of God for service is to offer lots of encouragement. We must give team members opportunities for real ministry, even allowing them the freedom to fail at times, while always offering plenty of encouragement along the way.

Here are some practical tips for affirming youth and ministry team members:

1. Listen, listen, listen. You may think affirmation is all about what you say, but it begins in carefully listening to others' joys and struggles. You have heard it said that God gave us twice as many ears as mouths, so we should listen twice as much. This is difficult for those of us who are influencers and communicators because we like to talk. But James reminds us that we should be quick to listen (James 1:19).

2. Encouragement requires empathy. The word *empathize* means identifying with another person's feelings. If a teenager, adult volunteer, parent, or staff member is going through a difficult time, you weep with them. On the other hand, if someone is celebrating a great event, shout for joy like it is your celebration (Romans 12:15).

3. Be a comforter with your encouragement. The more experience you have in ministry and with people in different situations, the more you have to offer. Comforting requires listening and loving (2 Corinthians 1:3–4).

4. Help carry the burdens of others. This is part of our calling as ministers and can bring great encouragement (Galatians 6:2). When you were called to be a pastor and leader, you signed up to sacrifice time, emotional energy, and much more.

5. Offer words of encouragement. This last one may seem simple and obvious, but many of us do not do a good job with our words. We speak up if there's a problem, but we're silent when things are going well. If those around you are doing a good job, let them know it with your spoken and written words of affirmation. Paul urges, "Therefore encourage one another and build each other up, just as in fact you are doing" (1 Thessalonians 5:11).

PRINCIPLE 5: LOOSEN UP THE REINS

Horses will not go anywhere if the rider doesn't loosen up the reins. When my wife and I were dating, she took me horseback riding. I think it was a test. We headed out from the barn, into the fields, and then came back around on the main road where cars drive fast. I was following her and enjoying the day until my horse turned sideways down the highway. I pulled back on the reins, which caused even more confusion for my horse. Horses do not fare well when the reins are pulled back; neither do ministry volunteers.

Some leaders have a hard time giving up control of anything. We think we need to have our hands in every activity. There are many reasons we struggle with this. We fear losing authority. We're afraid the job won't be done well unless we do it. Or maybe we're afraid someone else will do the job better than we can, and that'll make us look bad. We worry about the time it might take to hand off a job; sometimes it seems easier just to do it ourselves. Or maybe we've had a bad experience in the past, when someone failed to follow through on a job they'd offered to do. Finally, some of us are reluctant to delegate because we want all the credit. It gives us personal pride to think we did it all ourselves.

But we've already talked about the great dangers that go along with trying to do it alone. It requires a different mindset—one that focuses less on how to get the immediate task done most efficiently and more on the long-term impact in ministry.

To delegate well, we must relax, loosen our grip, and apply the following principles:

- Seek out qualified people. Loosening the reins does not mean mindlessly passing on jobs to just anyone. This is the Lord's work, and it needs to be handled with care. Make a list of qualifications and expectations for your volunteers or students. Choose the right person for the task.

- Show confidence in the people you've chosen. Be encouraging and allow them space not only to succeed, but also fail. Use any failures as learning opportunities.
- Be clear about your expectations. Make sure people know what you are asking them to do. There is nothing worse in ministry than unclear expectations. As the leader you want to point people in the right direction and give them a clear destination so they don't get lost down the road.
- Delegate appropriate responsibilities. It's one thing to ask one of the kids on your leadership team to make photocopies for your upcoming meeting. It is another thing to ask that same teenager to offer counsel to another youth who's contemplating suicide. Be sure tasks are delegated to people with the appropriate level of authority, trust, and responsibility.
- Don't specify exactly how every job must be done. Trust the person you select to accomplish the work in his or her own way. This can be difficult for some of us who always want things done our way. Remember, you are choosing a person you believe can do the task successfully; although offering some direction may be appropriate, you don't always need to provide a step-by-step guide for success.
- Provide encouragement and accountability along the way. Don't just assign someone a task and never talk about it again. Be a coach and cheer on your team members. Set up meeting times and checkpoints, so people feel encouraged and supported and you feel sure progress is being made. If you have handed off the discipleship of a student to a volunteer leader, check in and ask how it is going. End your check-in session by asking, "How can I support you?"

A new mindset for intergenerational ministry requires loosening the reins of control. We are not called to do it alone, but to partner with others in the dance of ministry.

The most profound example of delegating comes from Jesus Christ:

Then Jesus came to them and said, "All authority in heaven and on earth has been given to me. Therefore go and make disciples of all nations, baptizing them in the name of the Father and of the Son and of the Holy Spirit, and teaching them to obey everything I have commanded you. And surely I am with you always, to the very end of the age."

—Matthew 28:18–20

PRINCIPLE 6: UNDERSTAND YOUR CHURCH CLIMATE AND CULTURE

What comes to mind when you think of politics? You might think of Washington, D.C., and our country's form of government. Maybe the word *politics* has negative associations involving manipulation or being inauthentic. But I think there are certain "politics" involved in negotiating the culture of any church or ministry. Over the years I have made plenty of mistakes in this area. It's not something I was taught in seminary. I was trying to dance a routine I'd never learned—and I ended up stepping on a lot of toes.

We might not like using the term *politics* in reference to the church, but we need to understand that every church and ministry has its own culture. If we ignore this, we're in for trouble. And that's especially true if we're seeking to build a ministry focused on intergenerational relationships between youth, parents, and other adults in the church.

After making many mistakes in ministry relationships and doing plenty of reading on the topic, I've learned a few things about what it takes to ride your raft down the river of church culture. If you apply these principles, you're more likely not only to keep your job, but also flourish in the relationships that count.

- **Be around.** Most youth workers love being out among students, volunteer leaders, and parents. (Notice that I said "most"—not "all.") One reason we're in this work is because we enjoy being with kids—and that means spending time where kids are. As a result, there is this tension between "being around" the ministry office and "being with students." We need to be strategic about where we spend our time and how others perceive what we do. This doesn't mean we should lie, cover up, and be deceptive or sneaky. If you are working in a small church where your boss is the senior pastor, I would suggest finding ways to have casual conversations with him or her on a weekly basis. The key word is *casual*—not just scheduled meetings, but natural times when you can connect about what's going on. The same is true for larger church settings with more staff. Do your best to build relationships with other staff and key leaders. The staff around you may never be your best friends, but being present in the office (with the door open) is important. And it's especially important in building a youth ministry that's connected across the generations to the whole church.

- **Be aware** of what is happening around you. Youth workers who are young and new to full-time vocational ministry often have blinders on when it comes to the rest of the church. They think and breathe youth ministry and give little thought to the wider church. This can be a big problem. Don't disconnect from what is happening in other ministries of the church. Church bulletins, newsletters, and the Web page are your friends. Keep your head up and your eyes open to the events happening around you. Stay aware of how the financial giving for the church is going. Keep on top of the church calendar. If you are in a church with a larger staff, have conversations with other staff members so you know what they're working on. Don't think only about the youth programming. If you do, it will catch up to you and your job. Intergenerational connecting points assume you have others' interests in mind (Philippians 2:2–4). There are many other important things happening in the church besides youth ministry.

- **Be careful** not to pursue your own dreams over the church's mission. Many youth pastors go on to become senior pastors or move into other roles because of their dreams. Be careful here. You were not hired to pursue your dream or professional goals, but to foster an effective youth ministry within the overall mission of the church. Many youth pastors think they are operating on an island and like it that way. But thinking about connecting the next generation in meaningful relationships with older generations requires you to think outside the youth ministry box and to build broader relationships. Be sure to have lots of conversations with other leaders so you have a clear and complete picture of the church's mission and vision. With clarity, you will be able to navigate the waters of change and adapt your ministry to connect youth in intergenerational partnerships.

- **Be discerning** in addressing conflict. Not every battle is worth fighting—but some youth workers (young and old) seem to want to die on every hill because of their unbridled passions. Slow down. Take a deep breath. Count to 10—or 10 million. When conflict is handled with political savvy, it will end with stronger relationships. But dealing with conflicts poorly can be very destructive. Peter Scazzero has identified five unhealthy results of dealing with conflict wrongly.[8] First, the conflict escalates, gaining momentum. Second, the people involved in the conflict begin to withdraw from one another and possibly from the ministry. Third, one or more people begin to attack each other. Fourth, some of those involved begin to think the situation is worse than it really is. Fifth, "triangulating" begins to occur. People talk to "third parties" rather than dealing directly with the others involved in the conflict. Do not avoid conflict. Spend time with God, check your heart, confess sin, and approach the person you are in conflict with in humility and with an attitude of service.

- **Be a trust builder.** Nothing will help you gain credibility faster than building trust. And a lack of trust can knock you out of ministry quicker than any other factor. Filling the trust bank can take years, but it can be emptied in mere seconds. There are many ways to build trust, including having open and honest conversations with church leaders, showing maturity in your ministry relationships, handling conflict effectively, expressing humility, acting professionally, cheering for the whole church, taking responsibility, and partnering in ministry. If you remain silent and distant, the balance in your trust bank doesn't remain unchanged, it actually goes down.

- **Practice partnership.** Effective ministry—especially intergenerational ministry—requires assembling partnerships. Youth pastors of the future cannot build their own silos or live alone on an island. We need to partner with senior pastors and elders. We need partnerships with volunteer leaders who are in alignment with the mission and vision of the overall church and an intergenerational approach to ministry. Partnership with parents is a critical piece of the puzzle, given the profound spiritual impact parents have on their children. (See chapter 3.) If you are part of a larger church with multiple staff, it is imperative that you build relationships and understanding with those whose primary focus is on other ministries. With open communication, collaboration, and cooperation among all ministry leaders in the church, partnership will come easily.

The best youth pastors are students of the culture of their congregation and ministry. Every church or ministry has a unique set of traditions, values, and practices. Innovative and passionate youth workers often bang their heads against the walls of tradition without even realizing these walls are there. Take the time to understand what the traditions are, why they are there, and (especially) who put those traditions in place. Being politically savvy requires that you know whether a particular tradition was established by Aunt Betty who left the church years ago, or if it's an essential value of the current senior pastor. If you're thinking about changing "the way it has always been done," knowing who established the traditions could make all the difference in the world.

Take these suggestions to heart and they will help you flow down the river of church culture with more ease.

The time has come for those responsible for youth ministry to take responsibility for galvanizing the support of stakeholders in the youth ministry beyond the small circle of those actively involved in our programs.

—Mark DeVries, *Sustainable Youth Ministry*

THE PRINCIPLES OF EFFECTIVE INTERGENERATIONAL LEADERSHIP

1. Begin at the Bottom
2. Put People First
3. Build a Team
4. Recognize and Affirm Others
5. Loosen Up the Reins
6. Understand Your Church Climate and Culture
7. Get Out of the Box

PRINCIPLE 7: GET OUT OF THE BOX

Most youth pastors tend to be creative thinkers. It seems to be in our DNA to ponder new and innovative approaches to ministry. This is one reason some of us find it frustrating that we are rarely in the position of highest influence in our local church or ministry location. But we need to remember that God has placed us in a particular spot for a reason. We must be patient with those around us—even when we don't see eye to eye with our supervisor. Keep the principles of Scripture and respect the ministry culture around you, while strategically thinking like a "radical."

After all, it's often the radicals who change the world. Working from his garage, Steve Jobs cofounded a computer company that would challenge IBM. Chuck Colson went from Nixon's White House to a prison cell, but then went on to be an influential Christian thinker and writer. Lee Iacocca came from outside Chrysler and rose to the top, changing everything. William Carey was once told that his ideas about reaching the world for Christ were crazy, but he went on to become one of the most influential missionaries the world has ever known. Martin Luther nailed his principles and convictions to a church door and sparked the Protestant Reformation—flipping the church and the world upside down. The apostle Paul went from being a persecutor of Christians to the greatest evangelist the church has ever known, helping the first small group of Jesus followers grow into a worldwide movement of God. Martin Luther King Jr. had a dream that changed the fabric of our nation and our world. Jesus chose a ragtag group of fishermen, tax collectors, and everyday folk to be his first disciples—and you know the rest.

I am sure there are people of all different ages reading this book for a variety of reasons, but I want to take a moment to share something dear to my heart with any readers in their twenties. The current and future generations of the church will be led by innovative, risk-taking, creative folks like you. With respect, proper timing, and wisdom from God, dare to have risk-taking conversations with your supervisors and leaders as you seek to adapt new methods of ministry to fit the day, while strongly holding tight to the timeless and inspired principles of sound doctrine.

Who knows what the full future of ministry to the next generation will look like? We can't be sure, but I am convinced it will involve strong and intentional intergenerational connections.

STUCK INSIDE THE BOX

As you look toward future ministry, don't get caught up in the same old thinking, or you'll end up sounding like these folks:

There is no reason for any individual to have a computer in his home.

—Ken Olsen, President of Digital Equipment Corporation, 1977

I think there is a world market for about five computers.

—Thomas Watson, Chairman of IBM, 1943

There is no likelihood man can ever tap the power of the atom.

—Robert Millikan, Winner of the Nobel Prize in Physics, 1923

The photograph is of no commercial value.

—Thomas Edison, remarking on his invention of the camera in 1880

It is an idle dream to imagine that automobiles will take the place of railways in the long-distance movement of passengers.

—American Road Congress, 1913

Ministry leadership with a new mindset requires thinking differently and learning to make these principles part of your daily practice. Maybe you are well on your way with some of these ideas, but others need some work. Surround yourself with people who are further along on their leadership journeys and soak up everything they have to offer. Use this list of principles to guide your daily decision making in ministry to the next generation.

Here are a few closing warnings to spur you on to faithfulness in reaching and discipling the next generation. Unless you begin at the bottom, your leadership will be burdened by pride and arrogance, and your ministry won't last long. If you don't put people first, you will be missing your calling to shepherd the flock in your care. Unless you encourage those around you, your gas tank will be empty and you'll be stranded on the side of the ministry road. Unless you build a team, you will short-cut long-term ministry. If you don't loosen the reins and delegate ministry tasks, you will burn out in a few short years. If you fail to understand the culture of your ministry setting, your expectations will be unrealistic and your relationships will be difficult to navigate. And if you stay stuck inside the same old box, your ministry methods will dry up and rot, leaving you to do ministry like they did in the Stone Age. But place God first and follow the principles in this chapter, and your ministry will thrive.

True leadership requires partnership and humility. My seven-year-old son recently expressed the starting point well. He asked what I was doing on the computer, and I told him I was writing a book. Levi said, "Do you have your Bible with you for some ideas? If not, you can use mine."

That is the starting line. Use these principles under the authority of Scripture as building blocks for good intergenerational ministry leadership.

I am a dreamer. Some men see things as they are and ask why; I dream of things that never were and ask, why not?

—George Bernard Shaw

CONTINUE THE CONVERSATION

1. How do you define leadership in youth ministry?
2. How are you serving your volunteers, parents of teenagers, and ministry staff?
3. Which of the seven principles do you struggle with the most? How can you grow in that area?
4. Which principles do you think your team struggles with the most? How can you grow in that area together?
5. With whom can you share your creative ideas to get support for intergenerational ministry?

6
SHARING THE GOOD NEWS

EMBRACING NEW FORMS OF EVANGELISM

Compared to teens throughout the past 20 years, today's teenagers have the lowest likelihood of attending church when they are living independent of their parents.

—George Barna

If he have faith, the believer cannot be restrained. He betrays himself. He breaks out. He confesses and teaches this gospel to the people at the risk of life itself.

—Martin Luther

Each generation of the church in each setting has the responsibility of communicating the gospel in understandable terms, considering the language and thought-forms of that setting.

—Francis Schaeffer

Out of all the age groups, those ages 18 to 32 are the least likely to describe themselves as religious, as Christian, or as committed Christians.

—George Barna

Today, truth seems to be up for grabs. With digital technology increasing at super speeds, the definition of *community* transforming, and the dominance of relativistic thinking, the next generation is growing up in a climate where truth is questioned from every direction.

It is a new day that requires new methods. The central truth of God's saving love expressed in Jesus Christ will never change (John 3:16; 14:6; Ephesians 2:8–9). But our methods for sharing the gospel may need to change depending on the context of ministry.

The debate over truth is as old as the gospel itself. Pilate remarked to Jesus, "What is truth?" (John 18:38). Adolescents today are wrestling with that same question. They are intuitively asking "truth" questions as they wrestle with Identity, Autonomy, and Belonging (see chapter 2). They want to know if what they are beginning to believe lines up with reality.

Youth workers, parents, and other caring adults have the responsibility of helping adolescents answer these questions in an increasingly pluralistic culture. But there often seems to be a disconnect when older generations communicate the gospel to the generations that follow. The problem is not the message, but the methods.

Youth ministries need to find new ways of communicating truth to the next generation and in modes they understand. Certainly, our sovereign God is already drawing the next generation to himself even as you read these words. But we need to be faithful in our presentation of the gospel and help adolescents journey down the path of transformation, rather than becoming roadblocks that stand in the way of changed lives.

The simplest truth of the gospel and the profoundest truth of theology must be put in the same words—He bore our sins.

—James Denney, *The Death of Christ*

SHIFTING LANDSCAPE

The cultural ground is shifting under our feet. I am reminded of Jesus' parable of the wise and foolish builders. The wise builder digs deep and builds a home on a solid foundation of rock. The foolish builder sets his home on the sands, only to see it collapse when the storms come. Let's not let the moving sands take us away. Let us stay firmly grounded on the rock of the Trinity and the Word of God as we move forward (Matthew 7:24–27).

Most youth workers and other adults understand intuitively that the ground is shifting. We sense things are changing all around us. But let's take a closer look at these cultural changes as we think about how we can best share God's Word in these troubled times. I want to examine three shifts in particular:

SHIFTING SANDS 1: RIGHT VS. WRONG

Today, for many adolescents, the lines between right and wrong are hazy at best. All morality is viewed as situational. This causes choices of good and evil to be blurred.

When I was growing up, my parents made the line between right and wrong abundantly clear. If I crossed over that line, consequences would follow. Biblical teaching painted a picture of good and evil that was clear and absolute.

Today, tolerance is the dominant moral virtue. Too often this results in an "anything goes" attitude toward behavior. We can see it even in the simplest changes. When I was a kid, students got in trouble for passing notes in class. In this era of political correctness, they are "experiencing a sharing of lovingly penned meditations" by texting one another in class. Students don't get detention, they are just "exit delayed." Kids don't get grounded anymore. They merely hit "social speed bumps." When homework isn't completed or turned in on time, the assignment isn't missing but having an "out of notebook experience." Even when students are sent to the principal's office for discipline, it's not that bad. They are just "going on a mandatory field trip to the administration building."

Of course, I'm exaggerating. But do you see how switching the words around blurs the lines between good and evil? Adolescents need to be taught that God's Word makes a clear distinction between right and wrong. Understanding this and learning to live it out is how we grow into Christian maturity. Certainly, grace and acceptance of others needs to guide our living for God, but we cannot back down from the passionate pursuit of truth according to God's Word.

SHIFTING SANDS 2: MISSING THE BIBLE

There's a great deal of biblical illiteracy among the next generation. In the past even those who were not Christians tended to know at least a little bit about the Bible and its principles. Today, even within many churches, there's an extraordinary lack of biblical understanding among both adolescents and adults. It's amazing to think back on the past when politicians, teachers, parents, and coaches all tended to hold the Scriptures in high regard. I remember how my public-school basketball team used to recite the Lord's Prayer together in the locker room before each game—and no one cared. Times have changed.

I wonder if we've entered the time that the prophet Amos predicted when he said, "'The days are coming,' declares the Sovereign LORD, 'when I will send a famine through the land—not a famine of food or a thirst for water, but a famine of hearing the words of the LORD'" (Amos 8:11). Many churches and youth ministries today function more as entertainment centers than sanctuaries. As a result, adolescents do not grow up immersed in God's Word and in an intimate relationship with a living Father,

Son, and Holy Spirit. Many teenagers are turned off by church because they see hypocrisy in the older generations. The next generation of leaders needs to call the church back to a biblical foundation or we risk sinking into the quicksand.

On the other hand, although our biblical ignorance is disturbing, I do like the emphasis our younger generations place on community, authentic relationships, and worship. There are exciting areas of vitality among younger Christians today. With the Word of God coupled with the Holy Spirit's guidance, we can bring balance to doing ministry together among all generations in the church.

SHIFTING SANDS 3: PURCHASING POSTMODERNITY

Many in the next generation are embracing the negative side of the postmodern coin. The absence of biblical knowledge throughout our society reflects a landscape that is often labeled "post-Christian"—meaning that a basic understanding of Christian morality can no longer be assumed. Vaclav Havel declared it well when he said, "We live in a postmodern world where everything is possible and almost nothing is certain."[1]

I like Chuck Swindoll's analysis. He writes, "Instead of interpreting life honestly, people now interpret it emotionally. Instead of the real being real, people now distort reality, allowing virtual reality to take charge. Many among the younger generation *prefer* virtual reality—because actual reality is too boring."[2] This is a scary place to reside when a video game, movie, or "reality" television show is more real than a car accident or a birthday party. This is a new and challenging day. Youth workers, church leaders, parents, and other caring adults need to turn the tide by holding firm to Jesus Christ who is the same yesterday, today, and forever (Hebrews 13:8).

Media and advertising narrate for youth who they are, usually in ways that compete with the story of the gospel.

—Christian Smith, *The Youthworker Journal Roundtable on Kids and Youth Culture*

TWO WORLDS COLLIDE

Adolescents are growing up in a time when two basic worldviews are colliding. We still feel the influence of the modern worldview, a set of beliefs influenced by the Enlightenment that can be described as rational, religious, monotheistic, propositional, systematic, locally oriented, and individualistic. The modern worldview sees truth as objective

and understands reason as the way we get to this truth. Some of the adolescents you work with see the world through the lens of modernism.

On the other hand, many in the world and the church today have adopted a worldview heavily influenced by postmodernism. Pure postmodernism can be described as pluralistic, experiential, mystical, narrative oriented, fluid, globally oriented, and communal. Many postmodern thinkers disagree with the Enlightenment idea that reason can lead us to absolute truth. The most extreme postmodern thinkers would argue that there is no such thing as absolute or objective truth. They believe truth is in the eye of the beholder.

To be fair, some postmodern ideas suggest new ways to communicate the gospel to the next generation. Aspects like the mystery of the gospel, intense grace, the emphasis on personal experience, the importance of narrative, and a global focus are all aspects of postmodern thought that resonate with the gospel. We should not immediately assume everything about postmodernism is opposed to the Christian teaching. In fact, some postmodern thinkers are bringing fresh attention to parts of the gospel that have often been underemphasized. Much of the gospel is mysterious, and every evangelical would agree that grace is the very center of the Christian message. Experience, story, and global focus are critical for the next generation, and we can't ignore these aspects of the generations to come. I am not suggesting we should adopt every aspect of postmodern thinking, but rather hold modernity and postmodernity in the center of biblical tension. We need to pull the good, true, and right out of both cultural realities.

The challenge for us today is that we minister to youth who live amid this collision of modern and postmodern thinking:

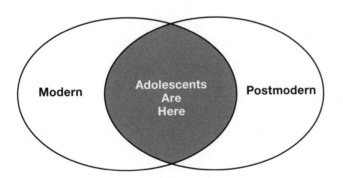

EVANGELISM IN A TROUBLED TIME

The growth of postmodern thinking, particularly among younger generations, creates a unique challenge when it comes to evangelism. As we've said, postmodernity is very skeptical about any claims of a universal truth applicable to all people of all times. Francis Schaeffer saw this change in thinking coming many years ago when he wrote about "the great evangelical disaster—the failure of the evangelical world to stand for truth as truth. There is only one word for this—namely *accommodation*: the evangelical church has accommodated to the world spirit of the age."[3]

We evangelical Christians believe that, in Christ Jesus, God has given the world an absolute Truth for all people in all times—and this is the heart of the church's conflict with postmodernism. You probably have already experienced teenagers who question (or simply reject) the Bible as the primary truth source. For them, the Bible is just one option among many and has no greater claim to truth than any other humanly constructed belief system. The next generation is growing up in a world where the voices around them are yelling, "You can't have a market on truth!" It is interesting that some do believe in absolute truth—but it is their own personal version of truth.

As a result, sharing the gospel with adolescents is difficult and a spiritual battle. They are hearing many different voices in a "me first" world. Christianity is not the only game in town anymore—if it ever was. It is just one of many belief systems. Kids are told to toss them all into a blender and choose whatever mix of beliefs suits them best.

Every few hundred years in Western history there occurs a sharp transformation. Within a few short decades, society—its world view, its basic values, its social and political structure, its arts, its key institutions—rearranges itself. Fifty years later there is a new world. And the people born then cannot even imagine the world in which their grandparents lived and into which their own parents were born. We are currently living through such a transformation.

—Peter Drucker, "The Post-Capitalist World"

IS IT ALL POSTMODERN?

Those who seek to follow the Triune God of the Scriptures run into this blender-belief mentality every day. There are modernists, postmodernists, and those who mix both, even among the next generation of adolescents. Even those who think of themselves as fully postmodern still tend to value logical thought and systemic analysis in many areas of their lives. Teenagers are doing the same thing as they organize their lives around home, school, church, the computer, the movie theater, and the mall.

I believe most of us are stuck somewhere between modern and postmodern. Some have said we are a generation of "depressed modernists."[4] We are not fully into postmodern thinking because we still believe absolute truth, yet all of our rational and scientific thinking and planning has failed to meet our expectations. As a result, we find ourselves in the space between the two.

Youth workers and other adults are stuck between two colliding worlds, and changing times require that we change our approach to evangelism. The message stays the same, but the methods change. This requires teenagers and adults to work together to discover God's way of living according to the Bible.

As they view the world through two sets of eyeglasses (both modern and postmodern), adolescents desire and need *experiential knowledge*. In short, they need to see real faith lived out by the adults around them. They need to see the Bible's truth expressed in human life. Shortly after I came up with the phrase "experiential knowledge" to describe a way of sharing truth with the next generation, I encountered the same phrase in Francis Chan's book *Forgotten God*. Concerning the Holy Spirit, Chan writes, "Many of us don't need more knowledge about the Spirit from a cerebral vantage point—what we need is experiential knowledge of His presence."[5] This is true as we share the gospel of Jesus Christ, but also in all phases of the Christian life. We need to share the truth in ways that allow it to be understood experientially.

The Christian faith remains real, but sharing the gospel requires more than mere facts or head knowledge. We need to move from the head to the heart. This requires a new level of passion for Christ from youth workers—in their lives, teaching, leadership, modeling, and discipleship. We believe that Jesus Christ is the "way and the truth and the life" (John 14:6) not just because we understand the facts in our heads, but also because we have experienced this truth in our hearts and lives. We need to find ways to share this experiential knowledge with future generations.

Christian theology is anchored not only to certain historical events, culminating in the saving career of Jesus, but to the authoritative apostolic witness to, and interpretation of, these events. The Christian can never weigh anchor and launch out into the deep of speculative thought. Nor can he forsake the primitive teaching of the apostles for subsequent human traditions.

—John Stott, *The Letters of John*

STANDING TRUE

Youth workers will need to be discerning, searching for opportunities to share God's truth while challenging the false views of the day. This requires an intergenerational body of believers who are grounded in the Scriptures and care deeply about the next generation. Let me share some suggestions for ways to keep our eyes and ears open as we seek to share the gospel with teenagers.

First, recognize that the extra emphasis today's generation places on personal relationships and conversations can open new opportunities for sharing the gospel. The danger is that when our focus is on having "healthy dialogue" and "fruitful conversations" about "spiritual things," we may neglect the truth defined by the Bible and not really share the gospel at all. We must be careful that our effort to respect people doesn't lead to a watering down of God's truth. The apostle Paul said, "Am I now trying to win human approval, or God's approval? Or am I trying to please people? If I were still trying to please people, I would not be a servant of Christ" (Galatians 1:10). We are not in this calling to please people, but to please God and partner with God to see the next generation come to a saving understanding of Jesus Christ. The evidence of this pleasing God is obeying his commandments and walking out the grace we have been given (Ephesians 2:8–10). Jesus said, "On that day you will realize that I am in my Father, and you are in me, and I am in you. Whoever has my commands and keeps them is the one who loves me. Anyone who loves me will be loved by my Father, and I too will love them and show myself to them" (John 14:20–21). There is certainly nothing wrong with having fellowship with others—indeed, we are called to build community and connect in relationships. But when we avoid sharing the hard truths of the gospel (in love) because we don't want to offend anyone, we are missing the point.

Second, some seem to prize tolerance above all other virtues. Certainly, there are differing definitions for the word *tolerance*; but when we land on just accepting any and every sort of belief in an effort to be fair, we are missing the point of the gospel. This can lead to universalism, which is unbiblical. The next generation needs to know that a powerful but loving God established boundaries for a reason. He loves us and sent his Son to save us (John 3:16). God doesn't put up fence lines to make our lives difficult or restrictive, but to actually provide more freedom for us to run around anywhere we want to inside his promises. The world just wants us to accept things as they are, but in his grace God wants us to bring change to the world and to ourselves through the power of the Trinity. Teenagers need to understand that God wants us to run away from evil, not "tolerate" it—because God does not tolerate sin. Jesus said, "What comes out of you is what defiles you. For from within, out of your hearts, come evil thoughts, sexual immorality, theft, murder, adultery, greed, malice, deceit, lewdness, envy, slander, arrogance and folly. All these evils come from inside and defile you" (Mark 7:20–23). The apostle Paul urged, "Hate what is evil; cling to what is good" (Romans 12:9).

Tolerating evil in the world is contrary to God's desires for us. As tour guides of culture, youth workers have a responsibility to guide adolescents on the right path. "Flee from all this," Paul wrote to Timothy, "and pursue righteousness, godliness, faith, love, endurance and gentleness" (1 Timothy 6:11).

Third, some people who influence the coming generations believe that truth is subjective and ever-changing. They believe all rules and traditions are human creations, established through discussion and conversation but outside of the guidance of the Holy Spirit, the Scriptures, and the lordship of Christ. The writer of Hebrews declared, "Jesus Christ is the same yesterday and today and forever. Do not be carried away by all kinds of strange teachings" (Hebrews 13:8–9). If this absolute foundation is taken away, our houses are built on shifting sands. It's not up to a group of people sitting in leather chairs at Starbucks to declare what is true about God and life. It is up to God who sent his Son to show us how to live and then inspired the authors of Scripture so that we might know the truth (2 Peter 1:21). Adolescents need to hear and experience a congruent message from a loving intergenerational body of believers who share the same convictions.

Fourth, many teenagers are heavily influenced by voices that suggest there are many different pathways to God. Students hear such pluralism through a variety of sources every day—at school, on television, in movies, with friends, and all over the Internet. Doing ministry together in the church requires us to teach adolescents that all belief systems are not created equal. The world does not like it, but Jesus himself declared that he was the only door to a relationship with God the Father (John 14:6). He also said, "No one can come to me unless the Father who sent me draws him" (John 6:44). This little verse is troubling for teenagers (not to mention adults) because they want to be in total control of their lives. Developmentally, teens are fighting for their independence (as we discussed in the chapter on adolescent development). To believe that God draws us to himself takes the authority away from us and gives it back to God. Yet even Jesus submitted to the Father's authority when he said, "I have come down from heaven, not to do my will but to do the will of him who sent me" (John 6:38). In the garden, just hours before Jesus was to die on the cross, he asked, "Father, if you are willing, take this cup from me; yet not my will, but yours be done" (Luke 22:42). Isn't it amazing that the Savior of the world would show humility and submission to the Father? We must help the next generation understand that a loving and compassionate God is worthy of our trust.

Fifth, many in this colliding culture base their faith entirely on emotions, great imagination, artistic expression, mysticism, and group dialogue. Understanding and living for God does involve experience, creativity, and community, but emotions and feelings come and go. The apostle Paul told his young follower Timothy, "All Scripture is God-breathed and is useful for teaching, rebuking, correcting and training in righteousness, so that all God's people may be thoroughly equipped for every good work" (2 Timothy 3:16–17). The future and will of God for every individual is not based on fleeting feelings but on the Bible's instruction that equips us to do good works for the glory of God. Adolescents have a host of emotions guiding their everyday choices. Sometimes these feelings take them to places they should not go and decisions they should not make. Youth workers need to come alongside adolescents and help them grow into their God-given gifts and use them for his glory.

Sixth, one of the good things about the current age is renewed interest in the spiritual side of life. In recent years words like *spirituality* and *spiritual formation* have become very popular both within and outside the Christian church. While I celebrate the renewed interest in spiritual matters, I think we need to understand where some postmodern thinkers are coming from when they use these words. Seeking spiritual power, favors, knowledge, wholeness or oneness with a higher consciousness is what the world is pursuing with "spirituality." When I walk into a bookstore and head to the religion section, there are a host of books on "spirituality" that have nothing to do with the Christian faith. Many of these books speak of an impersonal spiritual force that comes from within us—a starting point that conflicts with the Bible. As Christians, we know that God came to us in Jesus Christ to have a relationship with us. In one of his letters, John, the disciple who was closest to Jesus, wrote these words: "We know also that the Son of God has come and has given us understanding, so that we may know him who is true" (1 John 5:20). Our God has gone out of his way to make himself known—personally—to every human being. Teenagers need to grow in relationship with this real and personal God (experiential knowledge), rather than buying into whatever spiritual flavor is popular on a given day. Encourage your adolescents in their spiritual lives, but be sure to define *spirituality* for teenagers so they do not drift into wrong teaching. Jesus said, "Watch out that you are not deceived. For many will come in my name, claiming, 'I am he,' and, 'The time is near.' Do not follow them" (Luke 21:8). Leadership needs to be careful with the language we use to describe discipleship, and the next generation needs to be cautious about following after any god other than the One True God of the Scriptures.

Finally, in this day many people live for continual change. Certainly, change and transformation are on God's heart for all believers who are pursuing him. But not just any kind of change. The apostle Paul warned, "Do not conform to the pattern of this world, but be transformed . . ." (Romans 12:2). This is our calling to be holy, and we must help adolescents recognize that some things do not change. Jesus died on a cross once and for all. This is a historical fact and a changeless reality. Youth workers, parents, church leaders, and adolescents need to stand their ground and not give in to the pleasures and pressures of the current culture. This requires great discernment and alignment to the Word of God guided by the Holy Spirit. As Paul encouraged believers,

"Do not put out the Spirit's fire. Do not treat prophecies with contempt but test them all; hold on to what is good, reject whatever is harmful" (1 Thessalonians 5:19–22).

If you believe what you like in the gospels, and reject what you don't like, it is not the gospel you believe, but yourself.

—Saint Augustine

THE GOOD NEWS

The word *gospel* means "good news." And the Christian gospel *is* good news. If it weren't good news, it would not be the gospel. Simple, right?

Of course, the central figure of the New Testament gospel is Jesus Christ. And the Jesus we meet in Scriptures is powerful and compelling. British theologian and author N. T. Wright says, "The longer you look at Jesus, the more you will want to serve him in this world. That is, of course, if it's the real Jesus you're looking at."[6]

Unfortunately, many adolescents (and adults) prefer a Jesus they've made in their own images over the real Jesus of the Scriptures. We've missed the real good news because we don't want to face the bad news. The bad news is that sin has separated us from the God who created us and designed us for relationship with him. But the good news is that we have been saved by grace through faith based on the redemptive work of our Lord Jesus Christ (Ephesians 2:8). This coming of the kingdom of God is not the product of human effort, but it's God's answer to the human predicament of sin. We are separated from God and in need of atonement for our sins. Yet when we accept this free gift of grace—the gospel—we are born again by the Holy Spirit. As a result, we are part of the family of God (John 1:12–13; 3:5, 16; Romans 3:23–24; 6:23). This is the message we need to share with the next generation. *This* is good news.

But we must not forget that we are not the authors of this gospel. God is the Author of the gospel. He authorizes us to proclaim it (Acts 15:7; 16:10; Romans 1:1–5; Galatians 1:11–16; 2:7–9; 1 Thessalonians 2:2–9). God is the original evangelist who takes great personal investment in calling people to salvation through the Holy Spirit and his partnership with humans (Acts 10:36; 2 Corinthians 4:4–6; Galatians 1:6; 2 Thessalonians 2:13–14; Revelation 10:7). For youth workers and other adults, this takes the pressure off. If God is the Author, the One who gives the go ahead to share the gospel and who draws people to himself, all we need to do is share it with faithfulness—according to the written record of Scripture.

This good news demands a threefold response from those who hear it. First, it asks for "believing." The gospel is "the power of God that brings salvation to everyone who believes" (Romans 1:16). Faith trusts in God's grace conveyed in Jesus Christ (Romans 3:22; 3:26; Galatians 2:16; 2:20).

Second, the gospel is also to be received and lived. It is a place to take your stand (1 Corinthians 15:1–2). It gives life and sustains life. As we grow in Christ, God offers us life in all its fullness. The next generation desperately needs to understand this.

Third, the gospel asks that we hope, expectantly anticipating Jesus' return. Adolescents tend to think they are invincible; Jesus' return is the last thing on the mind of even the most Christian of students. Colossians 1:23 urges us, "Do not move from the hope held out in the gospel." This hope includes a very real return of Christ, the pardon of sins, and heavenly glory (Colossians 1:5; 2 Thessalonians 2:14–16).

The gospel is expansive. It stretches and includes believing, receiving, and hoping. God gives us himself so we can be fully satisfied.

The warnings of God's Word are more fitted to obtain the ends of awakening sinners, and bringing them to repentance, than the rising of one from the dead to warn them. . . . He who made the faculties of our souls knows what will have the greatest tendency to move them, and to work upon them.

—Jonathan Edwards, *The Works of Jonathan Edwards*

MESSAGE AND METHODS

Although we've focused more on some of the negative influences of postmodernity on adolescents (such as relativism, pluralism, universalism, and the lack of absolute truth), there are other characteristics of postmodernity that can shape the way we share the gospel in positive ways. Before you get too nervous, let me explain some of the ways in which a postmodern culture opens new opportunities for sharing the gospel message.

For example, younger generations shaped by postmodernism tend to focus less on the destination and more on the journey. Certainly, this has dangers if taken to extremes, but I like the emphasis on the journey with Jesus, not just the final reward of heaven. Don't get me wrong: I can't wait for Jesus to return and take us home. I look forward to the very real promise of heaven. But in the meantime, we are on a journey—

and how we live out our faith makes a difference in this world. This is a message that will resonate in a postmodern culture.

While adolescents shaped by postmodernism may be wary of absolutes, the positive flip side to this is an openness to encountering the truth that others have experienced. Today's teens tend to be less argumentative in discussions of religious matters and more conversational and accepting. Certainly, more can be accomplished when sharing the gospel if you aren't trying to "win" a debate, but instead are inviting them to a life lived in partnership with the Holy Spirit.

Similarly, many in the next generation are less "task focused" and more "relationally focused." Friendship is a high priority for them.

In past generations, local environments, towns, and communities were the center of attention. Today, with technology making world news more readily available, a global mindset is what adolescents are all about. At the touch of a keyboard or remote control, global issues are on the mind. The coming generations are not as focused on being heaven-bound as they are on inviting the kingdom to come "on earth as it is in heaven" (Matthew 6:10).

The narrative emphasis of postmodernism means teenagers do not want a few verses of Scripture shared as proof texts, but they want to hear the whole story from beginning to end. They want to know how it all fits together. In past generations, the gospel presentation often amounted to a few quick verses and a short prayer to get it done. Certainly, to come to Christ for the first time requires individuals to confess their sins, surrender, and pray to God. But coming generations tend to be process driven. They like the journey and need a full change of heart, not just a quick confession.

With these thoughts in mind, where do we begin to share the gospel?

AN OLD STORY FOR A NEW GENERATION

The heart of the gospel is unchanging. The old rugged cross will always be the old rugged cross. Jesus Christ will always be Lord. The path to salvation by grace through faith remains the same, but the methods must change depending on the audience. The message needs to be simple and clear, but where do we start today?

In generations past, human sin was often the starting point. Verses like Romans 3:23 ("All have sinned and fall short of the glory of God") and Romans 6:23 ("for the wages of sin is death") were used to set the scene. I am not suggesting that these verses are no longer true. But I am suggesting that we might choose a different starting position when sharing the gospel with the next generation of adolescents.[7]

Instead of starting with the "bad news" of sin, why don't we start with some good news? My experience with the next generation is that they are all too aware of the "bad news" of the sin and brokenness of our world. They have grown up amidst news of terrorist attacks, school shootings, wars, tsunamis, and earthquakes. They know about divorces that tear families apart, drunkenness that causes people to wake up in unknown places, and sexual experimentation that leaves you feeling empty inside. They don't need to hear more bad news—or at least they don't need to start there. They already know that part of the story.

GOOD THAT OVERCOMES THE BAD

I'd suggest that the beginning point of our message should be the beginning point of the whole Bible. "In the beginning . . ." God created the world. God, who has always been, brought this world into existence (Genesis 1:1). Notice that the Bible never argues for the existence of God—God's existence is a given. God spoke and this world came out of nothing. I have found that many adolescents don't know the creation story—or they've stuffed it away somewhere and assumed it's not very important. We need to return to the start.

The next generation is deeply aware of the bad news of this world. They urgently need to know it has not always been this way. It started out good. Everything God created was good (Genesis 1:10,12,18,21,25). The culmination of God's extravagant creation was the human being. And when that final day of creation was complete, God declared it all to be "very good" (Genesis 1:31). Adolescents need to be reminded that the God of the universe—who does not make mistakes—created them to be very special (Identity).

Adam and Eve were placed in a beautiful garden and had full fellowship with God. God loved them, and they loved God. There was complete and total harmony. This is God's starting point.

Certainly, this harmony did not last. Temptation leads to sin, which separated Adam and Eve from God. Their relationship with God and with one another was broken—and this struggle with sin shapes individuals and communities throughout the Scriptures. But after humans gave in to sin, the first words flowing from God's heart were, "Where are you?" (Genesis 3:9). From that point on, the Bible is the story of God's passionate pursuit to restore his created people to himself. Human sin disrupts the relationship, but God draws us back with compassion and love. The prophet Nehemiah offers this beautiful summary of the God found at the center of the Old Testament: "But you are a forgiving God, gracious and compassionate, slow to anger and abounding in love. Therefore you did not desert them" (9:17).

Ultimately, God's great love for his people leads to Christ on the cross. God provided the solution to our separation from him by sending his Son into the world as a servant (Philippians 2:1-11; John 3:16; John 13). Jesus' death on the cross is the sacrifice that provides a way for adolescents (and all people) to be saved from eternal separation from God. It was for the glory of God that Jesus would suffer and die for the sins of the world. In explaining his journey, Jesus connected his own suffering and death with the sacrifice of a lamb during the Jewish Passover celebration. But his actions would do away with the necessity of ongoing sacrifices. Jesus' sacrifice was once and for all. In Jesus, the bad news of individual and worldwide sin would gain a solution. He is the "way and the truth and the life" (John 14:6) that allows us to have overflowing life today and forever (John 10:10).

The next generation needs robust and passionate teaching on the cross of Jesus Christ. It needs disciples who can echo Paul's words: "May I never boast except in the cross of our Lord Jesus Christ, through which the world has been crucified to me, and I to the world" (Galatians 6:14). The cross is the only solution to the sinfulness of adolescents (and the world).

THE GOSPEL FROM THE WHOLE BIBLICAL RECORD

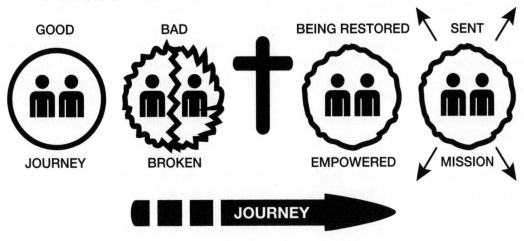

The Bible says that when God illuminates our hearts at conversion, he gives "the light of the knowledge of the glory of God in the face of Jesus Christ" (2 Corinthians 4:6 NIV). Either we see the glory of God "in the face of Jesus Christ," or we don't see it at all. And "the face of Jesus Christ" is the beauty of Christ reaching its climax in the cross.

—**John Piper,** *Don't Waste Your Life*

RESTORED AND SENT

As a result of the cross and God's free gift of grace, we are restored to full relationship with God and empowered to live a new life in alignment with God's teachings (Ephesians 2:8). When an adolescent is drawn to God through the power of the Holy Spirit and surrenders his or her life to God, he or she becomes a new creature in Christ (2 Corinthians 5:17). In faith, we become part of the family of God (John 1:12). Sin is still present in every believer's life; but through God's Holy Spirit, we are being restored to be like him daily. This is a "getting ready for heaven," if you will, where we will be fully in the presence of God and will enjoy him forever.

Youth workers need to teach adolescents that accepting Christ as Savior is only the beginning of the journey. Having been restored to full fellowship with our Creator, we are then "set apart" to grow in holiness for the glory of God. This is a goal to be pursued throughout our entire lives. Adolescents need to develop the same kind of passion and singleness of purpose reflected in these words of the apostle Paul: "I resolved to know nothing while I was with you except Jesus Christ and him crucified" (1 Corinthians 2:2). Believers in Jesus are on a journey to grow in grace that is progressive in nature. The power of the Holy Spirit is the driving force that changes us. This is a pursuit that we must pass on to the next generation.

So we have read about a great start of good news that turned to bad news because of sin, the receiving of God's grace through the cross of Jesus, and now a restoration to be more like him today and in the future. And, finally, we are sent back out into the world to share Christ's love.

Sadly, many evangelistic forms do not include this final push. Just as our shortened versions of the gospel message begin after the start—with the problem of sin instead of the goodness of God's creation—we also stop before the end: Jesus died on the cross, so now you are saved. But this is not where Jesus leaves it. Instead, he sends out his disciples to share this great news with the whole world (Matthew 28:18–20; Acts 1:8).

When adolescents (and all people) come to understand and embrace through experience God's plan for their lives, they become part of the mission to share God's rescue mission with the whole world—starting with their friends and family. To be a follower of Jesus Christ means you are passionate about the Passion. You want those around you to experience God's love and forgiveness for their sins. Youth workers, other caring adults, and parents cannot underestimate and underteach the significance of Jesus' commission for us today. Together, all generations are sent out to share this life-changing story of grace.

> I am convinced that only those who have made the effort to develop firmly rooted biblical convictions about evangelism will be able to overcome the cultural undertow of convenience.
>
> —Mark McCloskey, *Tell It Often—Tell It Well*

THE WHOLE STORY

We need to help adolescents understand the whole of the biblical story. By starting with Genesis and the creation account of "good news" and moving all the way through to Jesus' return to set up his kingdom as described in Revelation, we help students understand the full sweep of God's saving actions. We help adolescents see not just the story, but the way they connect to it. Their purpose on the planet then becomes clear—*to glorify God with their lives in the context of the church.*

The way we often present the gospel is like a child who opens a storybook in the middle and reads only a single chapter. He reads how the prince arrives on the scene, rescues a princess in distress, makes her his bride, and then leaves. But then the child closes the book. Later, he's left with questions:

- *Who is this princess?*
- *Why did she need rescuing?*
- *Why does the prince love her enough to risk his life to save her?*
- *What will she do now that she's been saved?*
- *Will they stay faithful to each other?*
- *Will the prince ever come back?*
- *What actor will play the prince in the movie version? (Okay, maybe not* this *question!)*

The abbreviated way in which we present the gospel leaves kids with the same kinds of questions. They hear that Jesus can save them. But they often don't understand why they need saving, what they are being saved from, or what they are supposed to do once they accept God's gift of salvation.

I hope you are catching the importance of sharing the gospel in new forms by using the whole biblical record with the next generation. We cannot compromise the message by failing to tell the whole story. In the sidebar box labeled "Summary of the Biblical Record" I've provided a quick reference of the broad strokes of the story of Scripture.

Use it with the adolescents in your care to help them see the whole picture of God's work throughout Scripture.

During one of his missionary journeys, Paul declared his passion for sharing the whole story, wanting his listeners to know the "whole will of God" (Acts 20:27). How much more should the next generation understand, during this critical time of their lives, the "whole counsel of God" so they own their faith? We should stay faithful to the whole of Scripture, knowing that we should not be ashamed of the gospel because it holds the power for salvation (Romans 1:16).

SUMMARY OF THE BIBLICAL RECORD[8]

Creation: It Is Good (Genesis 1–2)

Creation: It Is Very Good (Genesis 1–2)

Need: Separation (Genesis 3–11)

Need: Growth of Sin (Genesis 3–11)

Need: Nations and Languages Begin (Genesis 3–11)

Channel: The Patriarchs (Genesis 12–50)

Channel: Egypt (Exodus)

Channel: Plagues and Crossing Sea (Exodus)

Channel: Law (moral, ceremonial, and civil) (Exodus)

Channel: Wilderness Wanderings (Numbers)

Channel: Conquest of Canaan (Joshua)

Channel: 12 Tribes and Land Distribution (Joshua)

Channel: Judgments (Judges—1 Samuel)

Channel: United Kingdom (Saul, David, Solomon) (Samuel—1 Kings)

Channel: Divided Kingdom (Kings—Chronicles)

Channel: Judah Alone (2 Kings)

Channel: Captivity for 70 Years (Daniel)

Channel: Restoration (Ezra, Nehemiah, Esther)

Preparation: 400 Silent Years (Between Testaments)

Purchase: Birth of Jesus Christ (Gospels)

Purchase: Words and Works of Jesus Christ (Gospels)

Purchase: Death/Crucifixion (Gospels)

Purchase: Resurrection/Ascension (Gospels)

Proclamation: Holy Spirit and the First Church (Acts)

Explanation: Letters to the Churches (Romans–Jude)

Climax: Jesus Returns to Judge (Revelation)

FINDING NEW FORMS

The gospel needs to be shared within and across generations. Many adolescents have led their peers to saving faith in Jesus. Parents share the gospel with their children. Youth workers and other caring adults share with teens. Such intergenerational connections between older adults and teenagers are prescribed by the Bible (Deuteronomy 6; 1 Timothy 2:1–15; Titus 2:1–15). Older adults must be encouraged to take seriously the mandate of Christ to "go," build relationships with youth, and share the gospel message—whether through preaching, teaching, or one-on-one meetings where our personal and corporate stories of God's saving grace can be shared over and over again. The Israelites recognized the importance of connecting across generations. Central Christian worship practices like baptism and the Lord's Supper are very important in connecting older and younger people around the gospel. This is all good news.

Professional youth workers should not assume that the volunteer leaders and parents involved in our ministries will know how to share the gospel with their teenagers and children. We live in a day and age when biblical literacy is low, even within our churches. It is our responsibility to equip adults to reach out to the next generation.

Methods for evangelism are changing all the time. In the 1970s, evangelists such as Billy Graham were leading large "crusades" in which thousands of people came forward to make decisions for Jesus Christ. This approach made evangelism seem easy. Bring friends to a rally, have them pray a particular prayer, and they are in. Many churches adopted the "four spiritual laws" that were popularized by Bill Bright and Campus Crusade for Christ. (What is up with the word *crusade*? Is that really the era of Christian history we want to celebrate? Just a thought.) Many other churches were using Dr. James Kennedy's "Evangelism Explosion" as their mode for sharing the gospel.

Over time, the same kinds of strategies were increasingly adapted for teens, with large gatherings of teenagers and twentysomethings in stadiums who were invited to come forward, raise a hand, or pray a prayer as a way of acknowledging their desire to accept Christ as Savior. At the same time, new forms of evangelism were popping up.

For example, many Christian traditions jumped on board with Bill Bright's billboards and newspaper ads that shared the gospel. Later years saw an increase in evangelistic training events like those run by John Maxwell (now known for his writing on leadership) who helped church members learn to share their faith with his GRADE program (Growth Resulting After Discipleship and Evangelism). With his gifts and expertise in communication and leadership training skills, Maxwell had great success making evangelism "easy" for the average person. Strategies like GRADE were replacing the traditional altar call and revival movements.

Keith and David Drury are a father and son who are both ministers of the gospel in the Wesleyan-Holiness tradition. Their recent book, *Ageless Faith,* represents a cross-generational, theological dialogue that addresses many different areas within their theological camp. But I especially appreciated their thoughts on evangelism. I was intrigued by what David (who is in his thirties) says about the next generation's perspective on some older forms of evangelism:

> To us [Generations X and younger] it seems intellectually dishonest to think we can convert all kinds of different people using the same memorized rubric and four proof texts nested in a nifty acronym. It oversimplifies what should be a spiritual—even mystical—transition of the soul. Calling someone down to an altar to get a heaven ticket seems ineffective to [the next generation]. Door-to-door knocking, random witnessing, aggressive tracts, telemarketing campaigns, and competitive apologetics are tactics that seem downright offensive to lots of younger people. We think these methods might turn more people off than on. Obnoxious evangelism fits better with bizarre cults than the way of Jesus Christ. Maybe conversions chalked up this way are easier to count and celebrate, but many of us see no reason to keep this approach to evangelism. Conversion is more than making a quick decision—it is a journey to Christ.[9]

I believe David has summed up the feelings of many young people regarding altar calls and certain other evangelistic techniques. Personally, I am in favor of any technique that presents the message of Jesus Christ faithfully and invites adolescents to come to Christ. Only time can show the faithfulness of the resulting decision.

I think the key in evangelizing across the generations is to create a balance in between "experience" and "knowledge." Older generations get nervous about the word *experience*, while younger generations seem wary of the word *knowledge*. Many young people feel like certain linear forms of evangelism lose the mystery of the gospel, while their parents worry that, without objective truth, the gospel gets "watered down." As youth leaders, let's seek to balance the two. Let's not box God into our own system, but let's not ignore the facts of Scripture either.

For every teenager who comes to Christ, there is a specific point in time when that young person comes to faith in Jesus Christ. But there is always a story leading up to conversion, and a story of the life that flows out of that decision "event." Our evangelistic approaches must remain organic and fluid if we would be effective in bridging the generations and sharing the gospel amid the blurring of modern and postmodern influences. Let us never lose sight of the fact that, regardless of the form or technique, it is always God who draws adolescents to Jesus Christ through the power of the Holy Spirit (John 6:43-51).

The next generation desperately needs the good news of Jesus Christ. When youth ministries settle in and stop sharing the reason we gather as a body of believers—our common bond as a family—we have given in to the lies of the enemy. With grace and wisdom, we need to become passionately contagious and let this Tri-God's good news spread like wildfire in an intergenerational context from student to student, adult to student, and sometimes student to adult. Let's stoke the flame and present the gospel over and over again with fresh vigor.

CONTINUE THE CONVERSATION

1. What "tools" were used to bring you to salvation in Jesus Christ?
2. What forms do you see working and not working in sharing the gospel with the next generation?
3. Do you see the world as modern, postmodern, or a combination of both?
4. How do you think starting with the "good news" of Genesis 1–2 changes the way adolescents see the gospel?
5. What does teaching the whole Bible look like in your ministry to the next generation?

7

FROM OLDER TO YOUNGER

REVIVING DISCIPLESHIP TO THE NEXT GENERATION

And the things you have heard me say in the presence of many witnesses entrust to reliable people who will also be qualified to teach others.

—Paul in 2 Timothy 2:2

Set your faces like a flint, you have all power in Heaven and Earth on your side.

—The Evangelist in John Bunyan's *The Pilgrim's Progress*

So the word of God spread. The number of disciples in Jerusalem increased rapidly.

—Acts 6:7

Jesus came to save the world, and to that end he died, but on his way to the cross he concentrated his life on making a few disciples.

—Robert E. Coleman

On an autumn day near a lake off the back roads of Indiana, I took a group of twentysomethings on a weekend retreat to rest and listen to God. Before we left, I armed them with a number of spiritual "arrows." We dialogued about spiritual practices such as Scripture study, prayer, and journaling; and I invited them to fill their quiver with these "arrows" and then spend four or five hours with God.

They did. And so did I.

Our group took this journey as a way of learning to rest in God. The Bible calls such times "Sabbath rest" (Exodus 16:23; 20:11; 35:2; Hebrews 4:9). We called it a "Sabbath

Retreat." Like the rest of the group, I took full advantage of my time with God. It was a beautiful sunny afternoon. I began my journey by walking to the middle of an open field surrounded by a forest of oak trees. I stood for a while, then sat, then walked—all the while talking, praising, and wrestling with God. I took that opportunity to do some introspection of my life and recommitted myself to my life's mission statement. I asked God to reveal to me an "image" for my life's mission. I spent time basking in God's presence and admiring his creation, reading several books on discipleship and spiritual formation, reflecting on the people who had shaped my life from grade school through seminary, and thinking about the younger generation that would follow me. And in those moments, something happened. God revealed two words to my mind and heart. I began prayerfully journaling my thoughts.

The first key word God showed me was *sacred.* In journaling about what that word means to me, I wrote that I wanted with all of my heart to be "dedicated or devoted exclusively to a single use, purpose, or person, namely Jesus Christ."

The second word was *outfitter.* In my mind this was someone who had a "set of tools or equipment for a specialized purpose." My first thought was of those mountain climbing guides who have all the necessary tools to help others scale even the highest peaks. For me, in my role as a youth pastor, the word meant someone who "equipped or provided guides for the journey, namely for living the Way of Jesus Christ as a Christian."

Discipleship is investing in the next generation. Not necessarily waiting for them to reach out, but actively seeking ways to become a part of their everyday lives. It is making yourself available and opening up opportunities for younger generations to be included in ministry. It is walking alongside them as they grow, and lovingly teaching them.

—Mary, Church Leader

In those two words, God gave me the image I was looking for. I was called to be a "Sacred Outfitter," called by God to leave a legacy for his glory. But where did I start?

I started where any culturally savvy person working with the next generation would: I launched a blog where I could write about these ideas.[1]

While the specific image of a "Sacred Outfitter" was a new one for me, I knew it was all connected to something deep in my heart that was very old. And it surely didn't begin with me. It was a calling old enough to be on the heart of Moses in the Old

Testament and Jesus in the New Testament. It has extended through Paul and the other leaders of the early church, through countless other faithful Christians of the past 2,000 years, and down through the generations to the many faithful church leaders of our day.

For me, being a Sacred Outfitter is all about encouraging others along the path of discipleship. Some prefer the words *spiritual formation* or *mentoring* to explain this God-given commission, but I love the word *discipleship* because of its roots in the Great Commission. "Go and make disciples of all nations," Jesus told his followers (Matthew 28:18–20). *Discipleship*—that's what I want my life to be all about.

As we continue to develop a mindset for intergenerational ministry, discipleship must be on the heart of every youth worker. Older generations pouring their lives into younger generations has always been God's plan for his followers. There is no negotiating it. There's no backup plan on the heart of God.[2] It's all about making disciples. Let's spend this chapter unpacking what that means for intergenerational ministry.

Welcome to *Sacred Outfitting* Class!

Discipleship is living a life that glorifies and magnifies Christ in all things by loving, serving, and proclaiming Christ to others with humility and selflessness. And our strength to do this comes from being devoted to God's Word (our daily bread), listening to and obeying the Holy Spirit's leading, and prayer.

—Aaron, Local Church Elder

THE MASTER DISCIPLE-MAKER

When it comes to making disciples, Jesus clearly modeled what we are to be and to do. He spent three years preaching God's Word to the crowds and helping all who came to him in need. But most of his time was spent investing his life into a particular ragtag group of 12 guys.

No matter the size of your church, your particular denomination, or the demographics of your unique ministry, Jesus has provided a model for ministry. Youth workers need to be discipling a few select adult leaders and students each year so they can reproduce themselves in others. This is Jesus' model for how we will transform the church together.

Notice the words *few* and *reproduce* in that last paragraph. As we look toward a new mindset for cross-generational ministry, I think it's important to get away from the idea that each of us is called to evangelize the masses. Yes, Jesus does want the entire world to understand and experience his saving love and grace. But the way that happens is by each of us reaching out to a few who can then multiply. In the long run, this will have the greatest impact.

Imagine if you were to invest your life in just one key teenager over the course of the next year. Of course, you might choose to invest in more than one, and you'll also need to connect with the volunteer leaders or other adults who want to invest in intergenerational ministry to the next generation. But suppose, for the sake of this illustration, you were to choose just one youth in whom you would invest your time for the next year. Your goal would be to disciple that young person in the faith so that he or she was thoroughly grounded in God and equipped to invest in someone else, while you also approached another student.

You might think: *But then I'd reach only 20 kids!* Think again. If you were to follow this approach for the next 20 years, do you know how many people you and your students would disciple for Christ? Are you ready? You'd reach more than 1 million disciples for Christ. Is this hard to believe? Take a look at the numbers in the chart below:

DISCIPLESHIP MULTIPLICATION:

YEAR	DISCIPLERS
1	2
2	4
3	8
4	16
5	32
6	64
7	128
8	256
9	512
10	1,024
11	2,048
12	4,096
13	8,192
14	16,384
15	32,768

YEAR	DISCIPLERS
16	65,536
17	131,072
18	262,144
19	524,288
20	1,048,576

Imagine! By really investing yourself in just one person each year, you could have a hand in reaching and discipling more than one million people in the next twenty years! That would be quite a legacy. And this chart assumes that the youth worker disciples only one person each year. You and I know that we have more leverage than that. Most youth workers have the capacity to invest their lives in three, four, or five students, as well as three to five volunteer leaders. Imagine the numbers if we were each investing in six to ten individuals annually. They are mind-blowing!

Discipleship looks like a grilled cheese sandwich! When we are close to God, our insides melt and overflow into other places. We communicate with God. We learn to feed ourselves and are led by the Spirit. We see needs and don't ignore them! We develop a spirit of learning and growing, and an attitude of thankfulness.

—Ken, Youth Pastor

STOPPING SHORT OF REPRODUCING

My experience is that most youth workers are pretty good at event planning, programming, facilitating discussions, teaching, leading small-group Bible studies, playing video games, texting, and keeping up with their social networking sites and blogs. But none of these are the same as discipleship. Disciples don't just plan events and pass on information hoping something will stick. Paul gave us a blueprint for discipling others with his words to his disciple Timothy: "And the things you have heard me say in the presence of many witnesses entrust to reliable people who will also be qualified to teach others" (2 Timothy 2:2). Take a look. Paul (person one) instructs the younger Timothy (person two) to share what Paul has taught him with reliable people (persons three, four—and more?) who can then teach others (persons five and beyond). This is a deeply intergenerational approach to ministry. It includes adults and teenagers transforming the church together. It is a mindset for youth ministry that understands that all generations are involved in the spiritual growth of adolescents.

If we are concerned only with meeting with students and volunteers in weekly programming, leading them in an occasional devotional, and getting ready for our next big event, we are falling way short of transforming discipleship. When I invest my life into the discipleship of another person, I must be concerned about that person's investment in another . . . and another . . . and another.

There are four generations of disciples here in 2 Timothy 2:2. Paul invested in Timothy. Timothy invested in "reliable people." Those people invested in others. And on and on it goes.

Our tendency is to think we can achieve maximum return on our investment by focusing on the large group. We favor quantity over quality. We want big results and we want them now. But discipleship is not fast, it's not cheap, and it doesn't settle for a half-baked result.

Whether he was addressing a large crowd or just his closest followers, Jesus challenged people with high expectations. Understand, it was a blast to be around Jesus. I'll bet it was fun to spend time with him. But he was all about uncompromising commitment. "Whoever does not carry their cross and follow me cannot be my disciple" (Luke 14:27). To be straight, Jesus kept his message pretty simple. He challenged people to count the cost if they really wanted to follow him (Luke 14:28). And part of that cost was to reproduce themselves by reaching others for Jesus. For some who heard his message, the cost was too high and the road too difficult. The "rich young ruler" in Mark 10 is one example. Over time some disciples turned their backs on Jesus and no longer followed him (John 6:66). But if our heart's desire is to follow him faithfully, then we must take seriously Jesus' command to reproduce.

Many believers hesitate to make this fundamental commitment to reproduction. Satan tells us that we are not good enough to make disciples. But do not be fooled. It is not your goodness, but the perfection of Christ in you that qualifies you to disciple others. It is not what you know but Who you know. If you have died to yourself, then Christ will reproduce his character through you.

—Dr. Keith Phillips, *The Making of a Disciple*

THE REAL DEAL

Every so often I take a close look at my heart and ask myself: *Do I follow after Jesus like a close disciple or like the distant crowd?* Many are curious about Jesus but have no intent of being committed to him. Others are happy to walk beside the Jesus they've designed in their own image, but that "Jesus" doesn't resemble the Messiah of the Bible. Even in Jesus' day, many would hang around Jesus hoping to snag some free food (the feeding of the 5,000 comes to mind) or to see a miracle, but they had no intention of fully surrendering to the Messiah and growing in him.

How do we know if we are following close to the real Jesus? I think there are a number of "proofs" that show up in the lives of those who love him. As youth workers pouring our lives into those in our care, we should be looking for evidence of genuine hearts devoted to Christ. Certainly, it's not always easy to spot the real thing, but Jesus gave us a few pointers. Here are three that come to mind that I believe are worth sharing with adolescents as you do life together.

First, there's *listening.* The beloved disciple, John, tells us that those who follow Jesus closely know his voice (John 10:1-6). They are sheep who listen to the Good Shepherd. This involves reading and studying the Scriptures, as well as maintaining a moment-by-moment conversation with the One they love. Such careful listening requires open ears and a heart that is still. We must model and teach this to the next generation.

Second, there is *obeying.* Faithful followers do what the Master tells them to do (1 John 2:3-6). Disciples of Christ "walk as Jesus did." I remember as a little boy following my grandfather into the woods after a big rain. It was muddy, and I did my best to put my feet in his footprints. I missed his "holes" many times, but I tried to walk where he walked. Let's figure out where Jesus is heading and follow as closely as we can—and they help others to do the same. How are we doing at discipling the next generation of adolescents so they can walk with Christ?

Finally, there is *producing.* John tells us that disciples bear fruit (John 15:1-17). It is inevitable. Just as good trees produce good fruit, close followers of Jesus bring forth bumper crops during their lifetimes by using their gifts in service to others for the glory of God. The fruit of our lives are an expression of love for Jesus. Again, both showing and telling are required of leaders who seek to shape the lives of adolescents.

Following Jesus requires listening, producing, and obeying. Without these, there is no discipleship and the church is not transformed. Jesus fully prepared his disciples for the challenges they would face. It was not going to be easy. "I am sending you out like sheep among wolves," he said. "Therefore be as shrewd as snakes and as innocent as doves. Be on your guard; you will be handed over to the local councils and be flogged in the synagogues. On my account you will be brought before governors and kings as witnesses to them and to the Gentiles" (Matthew 10:16–18).

This might seem pretty heavy for ministry to adolescents. On the other hand, adolescents today are in the center of persecution and opposition in their world. As you share your life with a few selected adolescents, it's important to be real with them about what they'll face as they begin to live for Christ publicly. Jesus made himself available for instruction and encouragement as the disciples were going out to live for him. It is important that we do the same with the youth in whom we invest.

Discipleship is bringing someone alongside and walking with them for a time.

—Mary, Youth Worker

I believe there is a great opportunity for adults who are not formally involved in youth ministry to disciple young people—especially those of high school age and up—on a one-on-one basis. Because the relationship can be flexible, it is easier for people to manage than something that has to fit into a certain weekly schedule. This can, and should be, a mutually beneficial relationship. The older person gets the satisfaction of knowing and connecting with a younger person and the opportunity to see that person grow in spiritual maturity. The younger person has the opportunity to know a person with greater life experience who is not his or her mom, dad, or youth pastor and to gain from that relationship.

—Gary, Parent of a Teenager

THE HOW

As we think about discipling a small number of youth, we must give attention to the same three steps that we see in Jesus' own ministry. Our *selection, association,* and *instruction* should follow our Savior's example in ministry to the next generation.[3]

Jesus was *selective* about the people with whom he would spend the next three years of his life. The men Jesus chose were ordinary people—fishermen, tax collectors, and the like—but that doesn't mean he wasn't careful about who would be included.

Notice that Jesus spent a night praying for the Father to reveal whom he should select as apostles: "One of those days Jesus went out to a mountainside to pray, and spent the night praying to God. When morning came, he called his disciples to him and chose twelve of them, whom he also designated apostles" (Luke 6:12–13). This was an important decision for Jesus that had such far-reaching effects that we still feel them today. Shouldn't we take the same prayerful care in our selection of the few students and volunteer leaders into whom we'll pour our lives?

It is interesting to me that these 12 men were not alike. They did not have the same personality, abilities, or gifting. They were all unique individuals. The only thing they had in common was their Master Teacher. As you consider whom you'll invest in, don't look for kids who are all the same—in other words, not all kids who are athletes, or in band, or drama club, or "popular," or computer savvy, or attractive, or extroverts, or "perfect." Look for potential.

I do not believe the church is healthy unless younger people get quality time with older folks, and vice versa. They don't always ask, but they are definitely watching how we live so they can learn about adulthood. I learn from their wisdom because they see things in a fresh way. It's not about me playing the role of the older, wiser, in-your-face teacher; rather, I believe it's about growing together in the body of Christ.

—Lisa, Parent of a Teenager

Having selected *12* apostles, Jesus *associated* with them. "He appointed twelve that they might be with him and that he might send them out to preach" (Mark 3:14). Notice those words in the middle—"that they might be with him." Jesus doesn't just pick them and send them out to do his work. He's committed to spending time with them. This is why he doesn't take on 20, 40, or 50 disciples—he could not have devoted his life at such depth to so many. In a similar way, we need to make a commitment to "be with" those we select. Youth workers tend to stretch themselves too thin. This commitment to spend quality time with someone requires a tremendous amount of emotional, physical, and spiritual energy. This can be given to only a few. Such extensive association allows those we disciple to really get to know us and what it means to follow Christ. Consider what Paul wrote to Timothy. "You, however, know all about my teaching, my way of life, my purpose, faith, patience, love, endurance" (2 Timothy 3:10). How did Timothy know all these things? He knew them because he'd spent plenty of time with Paul. If youth workers didn't stretch themselves so thin by trying to be all things to all people, and instead invested their lives in a few students and volunteer leaders with the purpose of multiplication, the effect would be powerful, dramatic, and life-changing.

But Jesus didn't just *select* 12 men with whom he'd *associate* closely for three years. He took intentional times of *instruction* with them. He told them, "The secret of the kingdom of God has been given to you. But to those on the outside everything is said in parables" (Mark 4:11). The disciples were there for his public teaching, but they also had a backstage pass to Jesus' life, his ministry, and his heart. They got to see him when he wasn't in front of the crowds. How many youth workers allow those they are investing in to see them transparent and open? This is important. We need to "let our guard down" with those whom we are intentionally discipling. Of course this requires discernment and wisdom in what to reveal and when to reveal it.

But what about the content of the instruction we offer? That's where we'll turn our attention next . . .

I believe discipling isn't an option if you call yourself a Christian. I haven't been a Christian for very long, and I'm already seeing myself put into situations where God has called me to disciple others. Sounds easy, but it's not. I have found it's easier to live the sinful self-centered life than be a disciplined Christian. So how, you ask? By your example as you follow Jesus.

—Anonymous Blogger

THE CONTENT OF THE COMMISSION

Paul sets the bar high when he talks about the instruction he's offered to the elders in the Ephesian church, "You know how I lived the whole time I was with you . . . For I have not hesitated to proclaim to you the whole will of God" (Acts 20:18, 27). In his lifestyle and his proclamation, Paul sought to instruct disciples in "the whole will of God." But that seems huge, doesn't it? How do we begin to do that?

One critical way is by focusing on the goal. What do we want our young people to become?

In training and nurturing disciples, as in so many other tasks, it's easy to get so caught up in the moment-by-moment details that we never lift our heads to see if we are progressing toward the goal. I remember when I went out for the track team in junior high school. Everyone who tried out made the team—the only question was which event you'd run. I was a pretty small guy (just 4'10" by the end of eighth grade), and the coaches thought I'd be better at long-distance running. (I always thought little guys were better sprinters, but that is not what they thought.) So they asked me to run the mile. The first time I tried it, I took off sprinting when the gun went off. After just a few hundred yards I was exhausted, and I barely made it to the end of the race. I had no idea how much energy it would take to run four laps around that huge track. But over time, I learned to pace myself so I had a little something left for that final lap.

I will never forget what my coach said to me about finishing strong: "When you turn the last corner and head for the finish line, keep your head up. Look to the trees a hundred yards away so you cross the finish line hard." That was good advice.

Youth workers need to have the end in mind. If we don't pace ourselves and keep our heads up, we will not make it. And if we don't have a clear understanding of what we want young people to know and do in relationship to the Triune God, we will not be giving clear instruction.

We need to know where we want our young disciples to go if we're going to help them get there. I love the way Dallas Willard defines *discipleship* or *spiritual formation* as "the process through which those who love and trust Jesus Christ effectively take on His character."[4] Our goal is to help youth grow in the character and likeness of Christ—to help them become disciples and connect to the body of Christ as they move through adolescence toward adult maturity.

Christian discipleship is a process of paying more and more attention to God's righteousness and less and less attention to our own; finding the meaning of our lives not by probing our moods and motives and morals, but by believing in God's will and purposes; making a map of the faithfulness of God, not charting the rise and fall of our own enthusiasms.

—Eugene Peterson, *Life at Its Best*

MAPPING FAITHFULNESS

We need to help the next generation map out a path to faithfully serving God in their lives. As I've considered the characteristics we need to nurture in adolescent disciples, I've appreciated Fran Cosgrove's book, *Essentials of Discipleship.*[5] The 11 items on the list below were inspired by Cosgrove's work, and I believe they reflect the kind of characteristics Jesus tried to build into his disciples. As you read this list, start with yourself and then move out to others. Think first about how well you reflect these characteristics in your own life and what you can do to follow Christ more closely. Then consider how you might pass these traits on to the small group of students and adult leaders in whom you are investing your life. How can you nurture and draw out these items in those you are discipling? (See Appendix D for a more extensive list of traits, qualities, and skills found in Scripture that you can help develop among adolescents.)

Remember to keep the end goal in mind—to help adolescents grow in developmentally appropriate ways into disciples of Christ who are connected to the church. That goal is like the address you punch into your GPS when you are driving to a new destination. If you punch in the wrong address, you'll never reach the right destination, no matter how carefully you follow the directions. Think of these 11 characteristics as your GPS for Discipleship:

1. Teachable. Disciples are learners who are open and teachable about the things of God (Matthew 4:19; John 6:60–66). As youth workers, we need to talk about and develop opportunities for teens to grow to be more teachable and not self-centered.

2. Christ First. Disciples strive to put Christ first in all areas of life (Matthew 6:9–13, 24, 33; John 13:13). Jesus said, "Whoever want to be my disciple must deny themselves and take up their cross daily and follow me" (Luke 9:23).

3. Purity. The world needs disciples who are committed to a life of purity and who take steps to separate themselves from sin (1 Corinthians 6:19–20; Ephesians 4:22–32; Colossians 3:5–10; 1 Thessalonians 4:3–7; Titus 2:12–14). The next generation is growing up in challenging times, but we must help them live with purity and integrity.

4. Devotional Time. Disciples of Jesus Christ maintain a daily discipline of devotions and prayer (Psalm 27:4; 42:1–2; Mark 1:35; Luke 11:1–4; 1 Thessalonians 5:17–18; James 1:5–7; 5:16). Jesus modeled and taught this. We need to do the same with our disciples.

5. Apply the Bible. Faithful disciples seek to apply biblical truths in all aspects of their daily lives. The next generation needs help in demonstrating faithfulness by learning to apply the Word of God in a variety of settings. The Bible is our bedrock. We need to develop in ourselves and nurture in others the tools necessary to

go deeper in the Word of God through preaching, teaching, reading, meditation, and memory (John 8:31; Acts 2:42; 17:11; Colossians 3:16; 2 Timothy 2:15).

6. Share the Gospel. Many young Christians miss the importance of sharing the gospel of Christ with others. We need to help develop hearts for witnessing and giving clear testimony, so we might present the gospel regularly with increasing skill (Matthew 28:18–20; Acts 1:8; 5:42; Romans 1:16). As disciples of Jesus investing in next-generation disciples, we need to provide support to their sharing this great news. (See chapter 6 for more on this.)

7. Local Church Involvement. One cannot overstress the importance of regular local church attendance and being active in corporate worship (Psalm 122:1; Acts 16:5; 1 Corinthians 12:12–27; Colossians 1:15–18; Hebrews 10:24–25). Disciples need to be involved in a local body of believers. There are no exceptions, not even for adolescents.

8. Fellowship. Followers of Christ deepen their faith through regular fellowship with other believers. In this way, the body of Christ displays love and unity (John 17:22–26; Acts 2:44–47; Ephesians 4:1–3).

9. Serve Others. Maturing disciples of Jesus demonstrate a servant's heart by helping others in practical ways (Mark 10:42–45; 2 Corinthians 12:15; Philippians 2:25–30).

10. Financial Stewardship. Youth workers need to model and pass on principles that honor God with their finances (Malachi 3:10–11; 1 Corinthians 16:12–20; 2 Corinthians 8–9).

11. Spirit-Filled. Disciples demonstrate the fruit of the Spirit in their relationships with Jesus Christ and with others (John 15:1–5; Galatians 5).

GPS DISCIPLESHIP SUMMARY

1. Teachable
2. Christ First
3. Purity
4. Devotional Time
5. Apply the Bible
6. Share the Gospel

7. Local Church Involvement
8. Fellowship
9. Serve Others
10. Financial Stewardship
11. Spirit-Filled

If we have these traits in mind as we pour our lives into the next generation, I believe we will be more likely to develop disciples who are equipped to live faithfully for Christ themselves and to reproduce their faith by growing other disciples. We have to aim for the mark—and, with God's help, we will hit the bull's-eye. This requires an adventurous heart. As Duffy Robbins has written: "Christians were not called to be settlers; we are called to be adventurers, explorers, those who maintain pursuit, who seek to cover new ground. There is nothing moderate about this journey."[6]

Discipleship is a journey that is not to be taken lightly, but strategically. In the words of Nick Taylor, it is "a process concerned with the holistic growth and development of the individual. . . . not post-conversion maintenance. It is an ongoing path of developmental learning and experience."[7] Youth workers are called to this high place of serving the next generation with our lives so they might join with us as faithful followers of the Triune God.

RELEASING THEM TO DISCIPLE OTHERS

Jesus did more than just tell us about discipleship or give us good teachings to follow—although he surely did both of those. He also gave us a rhythm for dancing in discipleship.

Now, I am the first to admit that I do not have much rhythm. I have been called "stiff." I'm not a bad athlete, but I was never much of a dancer. My movement always seemed too mechanical—it didn't flow. But I've learned that when it comes to discipleship, we all must become daring dancers.

Jesus shows us the way to the dance floor. First, he begins by inviting potential disciples to "come and see." He invites them to watch his movements, to listen to his words. Jesus did not force people to follow him. He just extended invitations. As youth workers, we need to be inspiring, creating interest, and gathering crowds *for the purpose of discipleship.* That last phrase is the key. Gathering large crowds is not an end, but a beginning. Our big programming for youth ministry falls in this phase. The example of this "come and see" phase is illustrated in the beginning of John's gospel where a few disciples started to follow, but most were at a distance just watching and considering (John 1:39–4:46).

Second, Jesus moves to a "come and follow me" phase that begins the dance thatleads to full-on discipleship (Matthew 4:18–20; Mark 1:16–20). This is where the dance really begins to take shape. In this stage young followers are establishing a relationship with Christ. This is where our lists of objectives and results come into play with discipling the next generation. (Again, see Appendix D for an extended list of objectives.) Whereas the "come and see" stage reached out to the largest possible group, there is more limited participation in the "come and follow me" phase. This is where you might put out the invitation to develop a discipleship group you are pouring your life into. This requires some commitment from individuals who want to join.

Third, with the disciples Jesus moved to a deeper level with a "come and be with me" phase (Mark 3:13–14; Luke 6:13). This is typically quieter and more personal, and it involves a smaller group of young people and adult volunteers—but it is critical to your ministry as a youth worker. The goal of this phase is to take a few maturing disciples and help them become disciple-makers, too. These are the reproducers. We might wish that everyone would be reproducers, but in reality, there will be fewer. Those in this phase are empowered to do ministry alongside us. Note that this isn't just seeking people to whom we can delegate things we'd rather not do ourselves. We need to ask: Where are these disciples gifted? Release to them areas of ministry that match their God-given design and potential. This is a new mindset and requires smooth dancing for the sake of adolescents connecting with Jesus and the local church.

Fourth, in some of Jesus' final words to his closest disciples, he said, "Remain in me" (John 15:4–7). Knowing his time with the disciples would not last much longer, Jesus left these faithful disciples in the hands of the Holy Spirit. Those who had seen, followed, and been were now being sent out to do God's work. We must do the same. Send them out. Let them go—like a mama bird lets her chicks out of the nest or parents release their graduating high schooler into the real world. We too need to let go so those whom we have discipled can continue to do God's work while abiding in Christ's love. This takes the lead youth worker out of the spotlight. If we have done our job sharing "the whole will of God" with those few close disciples, they will be ready to be in ministry.

I've had the honor of being discipled by many faithful people over the years. They included my parents, Sunday school teachers, pastors, school teachers, seminary professors, itinerant speakers, and other leaders at my current church—not to mention historical mentors whose biographies I have read and, of course, the many faithful women and men of Scripture. I could share many different stories about those who have discipled me, but I'll tell you only one.

After my wife and I were married in 1994, we took a two-week honeymoon and then headed off to a new life in Columbia, South Carolina. We were a couple of newlyweds with a new outlook on life and passion to be trained for our calling of full-time vocational ministry at Columbia International University (CIU). Little did we know, this would be "holy ground." Our experiences with friends, other students, and professors were some of the pivotal moments of our lives. Not long into my seminary experience, I met a professor named Dr. William Jones. I began to gravitate toward his southern drawl and his deep love for the Lord. He had all the credentials to teach at the seminary, but he was really an evangelist, disciple-maker, and pastor at heart. His humility and compassion for people poured through his contagious smile.

I don't quite remember when or how it happened, but Bill invited me to be part of a small group of guys who met with him weekly for lunch. (He asked us to call him Bill.) I felt honored. Before long, the two of us began meeting apart from the group. He would share deep nuggets of truth with me like I was a friend and colleague, not the young, immature, clueless seminary student that I was. We shared ministry responsibilities at a local church; we had a season of accountability with each other; and toward the end of my time in seminary, he recruited me to come on staff in his parachurch ministry. My wife and I felt led by God in another direction, but I will never forget the huge impact Bill had on my life.

As the famous radio storyteller Paul Harvey used to say, "Now, the rest of the story." Today, Dr. William Jones is the president of Columbia International University (Bible College and Seminary). I feel deeply honored to have come up close to his life and ministry while he proactively discipled me during a pivotal point near the beginning of my own ministry. I have no doubt that Bill is the right man for that influential position.

Imagine what great things God might do if you take the time to pour your life into a young man or woman and then invite the one you've discipled to turn around and disciple others. Who knows what God will do in and through your ministry?

DARE TO MAKE DISCIPLES

Alister McGrath has noted that in the Middle Ages believers in Jesus were often referred to by the Latin word *viator*, which means "wayfarer" or "traveler."[8] Older adults, middle-aged adults, younger adults, adolescents, and children all have something in common. We are all fellow travelers. All of us are in process. We are each on a journey toward maturity. But the likelihood of a young person's reaching maturity in Christ in this lifetime goes down dramatically without intentional discipleship by older generations. If we want to build disciples, we must be faithful in our selection, association, and instruction of leaders from the next generation. This is not exclusive, but strategic for our ministries.

God gave Moses these words to write down and pass on to the next generation: "Love the LORD your God with all your heart and with all your soul and with all your strength. These commandments that I give you today are to be on your hearts. Impress them on your children. Talk about them when you sit at home and when you walk along the road, when you lie down and when you get up" (Deuteronomy 6:5–7). It is the same desire we hear in Jesus' Great Commission as he urges his followers to "go and make disciples . . . teaching them to obey everything I have commanded you" (Matthew 28:18–20). It is the same desire we find in Paul as he writes to the church in Colossae about maturity in Christ: "We proclaim him, admonishing and teaching everyone with all wisdom, so that we may present everyone fully mature in Christ" (Colossians 1:28). No matter how long an adolescent is in our care, we need to be faithful in passing on "the whole will of God"

so that he or she will become a reproducer of disciples. This is our commission and our calling—so it must be part of our intergenerational ministry thinking.

CONTINUE THE CONVERSATION

1. How do you "do" discipleship in your youth ministry?
2. Why do you think many fall short of helping others "reproduce" faithful adolescent disciples in their ministries?
3. What would your ministry look like if you intentionally selected, associated, and instructed young people for discipleship?
4. How can you use the "GPS Discipleship Principles" in your youth ministry?
5. What would it look like to train parents and volunteers to disciple the next generation?

The Parable of the Yepherd

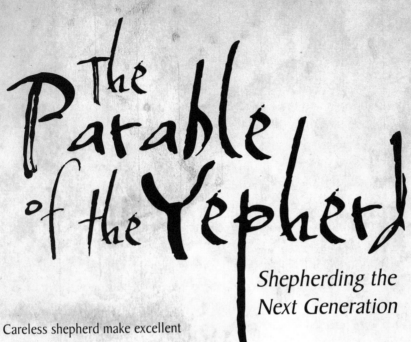

Shepherding the Next Generation

Careless shepherd make excellent
dinner for wolf.

—Earl Derr Biggers

Too many leaders act as if the sheep . . . their people . . . are there for the
benefit of the shepherd, not that the shepherd has responsibility for the sheep.

—Ken Blanchard

The LORD is my shepherd, I lack nothing.
He makes me lie down in green pastures,
he leads me beside quiet waters,
he refreshes my soul.
He guides me along the right paths for his name's sake.
Even though I walk through the darkest valley,
I will fear no evil, for you are with me;
your rod and your staff, they comfort me.
You prepare a table before me in the presence of my enemies.
You anoint my head with oil; my cup overflows.
Surely your goodness and love will follow me
all the days of my life,
and I will dwell in the house of the LORD forever.

—Psalm 23

There once was a youth worker who took his role in caring for adolescents very seriously. Following the lead of the Good Shepherd whom he served, this "yep-herd" cared for each and every one of the young sheep in his flock. The "yeep" had their own space away from the adult flock who were under the care of other shep-herds. The yepherd cared for his young flock and did his best to show compassion for them. His life's passion was caring for his flock—loving, guiding, and correcting each yeep, and always pointing them toward a deeper relationship and connection with the Good Shepherd. The yepherd had a balanced approach to his work—making sure to care for his own soul first so he could faithfully care for each member of the flock.

The yepherd desired for all his yeep to be content in their relationship with the Good Shepherd. He carefully led the flock to environments where they could grow and get living water and healthy food to eat. He faced many challenges in caring for the flock. Some yeep were tempted to wander up steep slopes or down into dangerous valleys. Some days it seemed impossible to keep the flock together with all of the distractions surrounding them. Occasionally, fights broke out within the flock. Other times, the yepherd had to devote extra care to one of the yeep.

If a member of his flock wandered off, the yepherd would leave the group to go find the one. And if he encountered a yeep who was lost, hurt, in trouble, or far from its own flock, he'd welcome that yeep into his flock. But his efforts weren't always praised. Many of the landowners who'd entrusted their yeep to him would complain that he was worrying too much about other members of the flock. Even the yeep sometimes seemed upset when the yepherd devoted himself to others in the flock. He had to prioritize, which left some members of his flock frustrated. It seemed that no animal was pleased all the time. This caused frustration for the yepherd. He was doing his best to make compassionate and wise decisions on the journey.

The more time he spent with his flock and studied them, the more he noticed that the yeep in his flock were not maturing as quickly as he'd hoped. Helping the flock cope with all the challenges that surrounded them often seemed to be more than the yepherd could do alone. They would get their hooves stuck in rocks, get lost or pulled away from the other yeep, or fall and would require help to get back up again. The yepherd did his best to care for the entire flock, but the demands were too great.

Some of the landowners were helpful. They recognized that the yepherd could not possibly meet the needs of every member of the flock. Sometimes they would accompany the yepherd as he cared for the flock. But other landowners seemed to show very little interest in what happened to the flock.

The yepherd did his best to find nourishing food for the flock, while battling against wolves and other dangers. But there were outside forces and inside forces that distracted the yeep. The yepherd's vision for helping the yeep grow and mature seemed to differ from the vision of some landowners. On some level the yepherd felt he'd been given responsibility for the flock, but not the support to truly care for them.

One day, the yepherd fell asleep and he had a dream. He realized he could not possibly give his young flock all that they needed to grow and thrive. He needed help from the other shepherds. His young flock needed to be around mature sheep. He needed the supportive presence of the landowners who'd entrusted their young to his care. The yepherd knew what he needed to do. He needed to surround each and every yeep with other mature sheep and caring shepherds. He needed the input and involvement of the landowners, since the yeep belonged to them and they were the ones most responsible for their care. The yepherd knew his young flock would never mature if he were the only one looking out for them.

So the yepherd began to share his vision with other shepherds and with the landowners, gaining support and trust. He sought out mature sheep that could walk alongside his young ones, helping the yeep find green pastures and stay away from the steep slopes. And with a network of care surrounding the young flock with love, support, and care, the yeep grew strong in their connection to the Good Shepherd.

Everyone began to take notice and look out for the flock.
Everyone began to care for each yeep.
Everyone kept their eyes and ears open so they could rescue any yeep in trouble.
Everyone took an interest in the next generation of yeep, knowing the future of the entire land depended on offering caring support for the young ones.

The flock grew and thrived because each and every yeep was cared for—not just by the yepherd, but also by others throughout the land who were offering the same instructions and love. There was a community of support for his flock that was much larger than he could offer on his own.

Some still complained that the yepherd wasn't doing his job. How come he no longer took the young flock off to a pasture by themselves? Yet no one could argue that the flock was growing and maturing. And the yepherd persevered because he knew that having a loving community that would surround every young one was not just his idea. It was an idea that springs from the very heart of the Good Shepherd himself, who wants the best for every single one of his sheep.

CONTINUE THE CONVERSATION

1. What does shepherding youth look like in your ministry context?
2. Is this a fair assessment of youth ministry today?
3. How are you connecting the next generation to the full body of Christ today (not just when they graduate from youth ministry)?

CONCLUSION: TRANSFORMING THE CHURCH TOGETHER

GAINING A NEW MINDSET
FOR INTERGENERATIONAL MINISTRY

Even when I am old and gray,
do not forsake me, my God,
till I declare your power to the next generation,
your mighty acts to all who are to come.

—Psalm 71:18

Dancing is the art of getting your feet out of the way faster than your
partner can step on them.

—Author Unknown

Your attitude (thinking) should be the same as that of Christ Jesus.

—Paul in Philippians 2:5 (NIV)

Intergenerational ministry is not like doing math, engineering, geometry, or biochemistry. It is more like painting, writing, or watching the sunset over the snowcapped Colorado mountains. It's much more of an art than a science. It is not a puzzle to figure out systematically, but a dance in which all generations join with God by participating in his original plan. It starts with parents who stay involved in the lives of their adolescent children, and it moves out to youth workers, ministry volunteers, and other caring adults. When it all comes together, we end up standing in awe of how God works

147

among us. And we are reminded that it really does take a whole village, a whole tribe, a community of loving adults to raise an adolescent.

This new mindset for ministering to youth and young adults is really about faithful shepherding that brings people together across the generations. It is about a whole priesthood of adult believers "pastoring" a group of young people. It is about young people who offer freshness, vitality, and new energy to the church. It is about people of all ages in ministry together.

I mentioned in the Introduction that different denominations, academic institutions, and ministry groups have been discussing intergenerational ministry for many years. Unfortunately, it is all too common for churches and ministries to miss the ways in which an intergenerational approach reshapes all we do. Too often, we talk about how it's important to connect the generations, but then we fall back into the same old daily grind.

We need a new way of thinking. Church leaders need to be reminded of specific areas that get reshaped when we adopt an intergenerational approach. Each of the chapters in this book addresses a theme that everyone ministering to youth and young adults should be meditating on regularly. These topics—adolescent development, family, leadership, culture, evangelism, and discipleship—should always be part of the conversation as we seek to minister with an intergenerational mindset for ministry.

Remember the image we used at the beginning of the book? We talked about how each of the areas we've addressed in this book is a lens through which we view ministry. When those lenses are not aligned, our vision is blurry and our thinking unfocused:

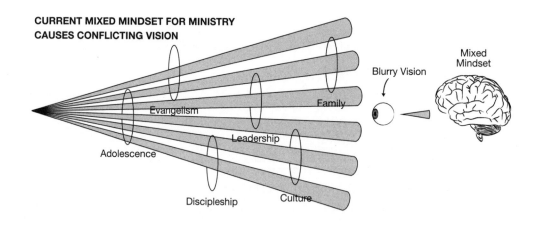

CURRENT MIXED MINDSET FOR MINISTRY CAUSES CONFLICTING VISION

Evangelism

Family

Leadership

Adolescence

Discipleship

Culture

Blurry Vision

Mixed Mindset

But when we get the lenses lined up, we get a clear vision for ministry. And with that new focus, we're able to minister with a new mindset that brings adolescents and adults together for God's kingdom:

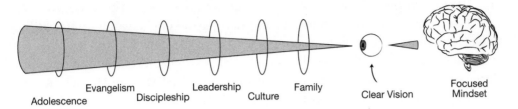

NEW FOCUSED MINDSET FOR INTERGENERATIONAL MINISTRY

Adolescence • Evangelism • Discipleship • Leadership • Culture • Family • Clear Vision • Focused Mindset

ALIGNED LENSES FOR CLEAR VISION

What you have found in this book is a new mindset for ministry. At first it may feel very odd to think about all these areas in a different way. It's like your first time wearing a new pair of glasses; at first, it may seem like your vision is even fuzzier. But over time, you develop the ability to see in a new way and with more clarity than before.

And here's the really amazing thing: The more you develop this new mindset for ministry, the less you have to think about it. Ironic? Maybe. But as an intergenerational approach to ministry becomes a habit, you no longer need to think about it constantly. It becomes natural. It's part of your ministry DNA.

The fact is, teenagers *need* adults in their lives—multiple adults. But the church also needs teenagers. Blue Hairs need Kindergarteners; Teenagers need Empty Nesters; Twentysomethings need Boomers. We're all the church, like it or not, and the *choice* to like it is a critical one. Isolated youth groups have done just as much harm as good. Isolation might make things easier in some ways, but striving for the best is rarely easy. Work to find meaningful ways for intergenerational community and relationships.

—Mark Oestreicher, *Youth Ministry 3.0*

CHANGING YOUR MIND

In my research for this book, I ran across Carol S. Dweck's research in the area of "changing mindsets." Dweck is a professor of psychology at Stanford University and one of the world's leading researchers in the field of motivation. In her book *Mindset,* Dweck explains that when it comes to areas like attitude and personal growth, some people have a "fixed mindset" while others have a "growth mindset."[1] She writes that those with a "fixed mindset" tend to want to look smart, avoid challenges, give up easily, see making an effort as a waste of time, ignore useful negative feedback, and feel threatened by the success of others. This fixed mindset leads to a person plateauing early in life and never reaching his or her potential. I have seen this firsthand and have heard many stories of this happening with youth pastors (and other pastors) in local churches.

On the other hand, someone who has a "growth mindset" is always seeking to learn and grow. These folks soak up new information like a sponge soaks up water. They are teachable and have an attitude that is positive. Dweck says people with a "growth mindset" have the following characteristics: They embrace change, persevere in the face of setbacks, see effort as the path to becoming proficient, learn from constructive criticism, and draw lessons and inspiration from the successes of others.

Even though this sociological research is not focused on faith, I found it helpful as we approach changing our minds for ministry to adolescents. The characteristics of a growth mindset line up well with biblical theology and praxis of ministry. I am hopeful that you have a "growth mindset," embracing a change in your thinking both personally and as a minister for the future. And we should always remember that, ultimately, as believers in Jesus Christ, our thinking (or attitude or mindset) should be the same as that of Christ Jesus who humbled himself serving the world with his death on the cross (Philippians 2:5).

There is a sense in which you can't just reform the "youth ministry" without considering how the other ministries in the church need to be intergenerational.

—Didi, Youth Pastor

STOP SEGREGATING EVERYTHING

We've already discussed the overwhelming statistics that suggest we're not attracting adolescents to our local churches, and we're not keeping them once they arrive. I am convinced that one of the primary problems is the way churches segregate our youth. The field of youth ministry exists because churches recognized that adolescence was a unique phase of development (or at least they knew teenagers were different). With good intentions and recognizing that teenagers needed special attention, churches began segregating teens to their own classroom away from the adults and children, and they hired individuals whose specific job was to spend time with teenagers. Before long, age-specific programming became the norm not just on Sunday mornings, but throughout the life of the church. On the one hand, this makes sense—yet it has fueled a great deal of dysfunction.

Connecting the next generation with older Trinity-following adults is critical to their spiritual depth and growth, but it does not seem to be happening.

—Kim, Parent of a Teenager

It's not unlike what happens at many family gatherings. There was a time when our extended family could gather around a single dinner table. But after my three older siblings and I all got married and began having children, many holidays were packed with a full house of at least 20 people of all ages. Inevitably, the dinner seating got separated into two groups—the children and the adults. At mealtime, the children would eat in one room (usually at a card table with folding chairs), while the adults gathered in the dining room. This was a break for the adults, if not so much for the older children (who were told to "watch" the younger ones so they didn't stick corn up their noses). There is nothing really wrong with this kind of separation from time to time, but our churches have been doing it every week for decades. Hour after hour, teenagers barely see, talk to, or interact with adults *in the church.*

In an article that raises questions about such separation within the church, Kara Powell executive director of the Fuller Youth Institute of Fuller Theological Seminary says, "The future of youth ministry is intergenerational."[2] I agree, but I believe our new mindset calls for a balance between programming specifically intended for youth and programming that involves the entire church across generational lines. And I think we have to place special emphasis on partnering with parents to accomplish discipleship.

Too often I think our youth ministries have been theologically shallow and developmentally careless. We've failed to understand the implications of lengthening adolescence and have caved to the cultural pressures that keep youth separate from adults while simultaneously causing them to grow up too fast. As a result, assimilation into the full body of Christ is too often an afterthought. Without thinking strategically about the changing culture and lengthening of adolescence, we failed to help our young people become part of the body of Christ in the here and now, instead thinking that "one day" they'll grow up and become part of the family. This is why I believe churches need to develop intergenerational connecting points where youth are treated as an essential part of the healthy functioning body, rather than just a hangnail, on a finger.

To foster intergenerational relationships in youth ministry would first be to promote the necessity of that idea to our church leaders and senior pastor. The hurdle I face is the acceptance of the division of generations in the church. I find no biblical foundation for such division but feel it is a societal following that has caused that division to exist within the church itself. I need to present the need to the leadership team and pray they will be open to bridging the gap that has taken a foothold in the church. I have done this throughout the past; but as of this point, we still do not have an active plan to bring generations together.

—Mary, Youth Worker

GIVE THEM SPACE (WITH ADULTS)

As I've said, I'm not advocating a shift in which all individual youth programming is eliminated. It's still appropriate for teenagers to have their own space within the church, but it should be in balance with adult interaction and love in the context of the whole body of believers. But we must also create opportunities for different generations to connect and share their stories of faith in God with one another.

As we think about making the church a place that will help adolescents mature into adult believers, it's helpful to acknowledge that people of all ages need several different kinds of space. Author Joseph Myers has talked about four types of spaces that surround every human being.[3] First, there is *public* space. This is space in which there are 12 or more feet between us and other humans. Depending on the size and structure of your church, many adolescents may interact with older generations only in the public space. The next level is *social* space, in which others are between four and twelve feet away. While it is common for the adolescents in our ministries to interact with one another in such social space, it is imperative that we also create opportunities for adolescents and Jesus-following adults to interact in social space. Ideally, we would like adolescents to develop relationships with older adults that move into the third category of *personal* space. This is 18 inches to 4 feet in distance. This allows for healthy boundaries yet is still close enough to build authentic community.

The fourth and final space Myers talks about is known as *intimate* space, and involves less than 18 inches between people. Certainly, marriage operates within this space, but many "best friends" will hug and embrace in the intimate space. Close family relationships enter intimate space. Certainly, intimacy involves a level of trust, and abuse of such trust can be very damaging. Yet imagine an intergenerational church family where appropriate and healthy intimacy grows across generational lines. This is a community in which all are loved and cared for as God intended.

Human beings were created for relationships—and a healthy network of human relationships includes all four spaces within the guidelines God has given us. Adolescents are in a developmental stage where they are learning to negotiate these four spaces. Intergenerational ministry requires that adults lead and model for adolescents healthy public, social, personal, and intimate spaces. Real Christian community between adolescents and older adults depends on this.

Sometimes we youth workers expect authentic community and connections between older generations and adolescents to come quickly. We want it to be like a Google search, where we type in "community" and it occurs in the blink of an eye. But it takes time and effort, and it also requires intentional planning, care, and patience. Mark Cannister, professor at Gordon College, has pointed out how the immediacy of the Internet causes young people to expect instant gratification in every area of their lives. He notes that this can be dangerous in areas such as relationships, academics, and sports.[4] It can also be a concern when it comes to creating space for older adults and teenagers to connect. Yet we must give these connections time to develop into true community. Francis Schaeffer brings conviction when he writes, "Our relationship with each other is the criterion the world uses to judge whether our message is truthful—Christian community is the final apologetic."[5]

[Youth workers need to] quit focusing on righteousness and teach youth to trust Jesus in every aspect of their lives. All sin is the unwillingness to trust Christ. Discipleship is being reminded that their identity is rooted in theology. Who they are is answered by letting them know Jesus particularly created them, died for them and called them. He does all of that while they're located in community. Trust Jesus and trust the people Jesus calls His body. As we do that, kids will discover who they are. Their identities will be formed as beloved children of God.

—Dr. Chap Clark, *The Youthworker Journal Roundtable on Kids and Youth Culture*

NEW MINDSET REQUIRES NEW GOAL

Leadership guru Stephen Covey has encouraged leaders to "start with the end in mind." This is true for building an intergenerational vision for ministry. We're seeking a different kind of end result. Youth workers need to move away from offering a mass-produced faith for all to a customized faith development with every student in our care.

We are shepherds seeking to follow the lead of the Good Shepherd in the way we care for the youth of the church. Each and every sheep has a name and a unique God-given design. Each of them has a unique relationship with the God who created them all. We need many adults surrounding each individual teenager to customize their faith development. Certain key components will still be part of spiritual formation in every adolescent, including time in God's Word, unbroken fellowship with the Father, and living in obedience and grace while building faith. But each faith journey is unique. We can't minister in an individualized way if we operate only within large-group youth program settings. We need mature Trinity-following adults willing to invest their lives in individual teenagers (not just small-group environments).

At Foothills Bible Church where I serve, our student ministry includes junior high, senior high, and college students—the full range of adolescence. We operate with a clear intergenerational mindset and the following mission: "We exist to help students on the journey to becoming mature Jesus-following adults who are connected to the church family." We have intentionally moved away from a mission statement that's focused on getting adolescents saved or "fully devoted." Intergenerational ministry takes us to deeper places of connection with the whole body of Christ. It means doing ministry together rather than in isolation. It moves us to deeper discipleship with people of all generations.

I recently was interviewed about the future of youth ministry and was asked, "Where would you like to see youth ministry in 30 years?" My answer shocked even me: "I am not sure I want there to be any youth pastors anymore." What I meant is that we have to switch the priority FROM the family as the primary spiritual formation model to the church . . . Let's get back to less programs and more training of families.

—**Dr. David Olshine, Professor of Youth Ministry, Columbia International University**

Note that our mission statement doesn't say that we grow students into mature disciples. We help them. God does the growing, and we have the privilege of helping. This takes the pressure off. We know that adolescents are on a journey in relationship with the Triune God. We need to help them deepen their understanding through our teaching and modeling. We desire for them to mature in their faith development, as well as in their natural psychosocial development. This requires many older adults who are present in the lives of adolescents, helping each one to mature and develop. Finally, the goal is each individual's full connection in a local body of believers that is intergenerational—a community that includes babies, children, families of all shapes and sizes, teenagers, young adults, single people, married folks, middle adults, and gray-hairs with lots of godly wisdom and life experience. This is full assimilation into the body of Christ today!

Interaction throughout the week involves all four spaces discussed earlier. Believers of all ages participate in a visible public assembly of worship where there is prayer, teaching from the Word, and fellowship. We celebrate the Lord's Supper and baptism, and participate in the organization, function, and governing of this local body of believers. The gospel is preached with life and vitality.[6] As Dietrich Bonhoeffer, a great follower of Christ from a past generation, once put it: "The Body of Christ becomes visible to the world in the congregation gathered round the Word and Sacrament."[7] Bonhoeffer understood the purpose of the local family of God. Adolescents need to be guided into connection with the whole of the church. Current and future leaders in youth ministry must look beyond "getting kids saved" and "plugging kids into the weekly youth program" to full-on deep discipleship and connection to an intergenerational body of believers who live out God's saving grace together.

At the moment I am trying to deconstruct the perceptions in my parish that older people are too old, the gap is too big, and young people don't want older people around. I am also trying to deconstruct the idea that youth ministry is all about the youth group or the youth event (programs). When older people and even some adults view youth ministry in this way, they tend to think they can't "run around with teenagers" or keep up with the energy—or it just seems too overwhelming for them. Relationships are the key, as well as broadening our understanding of youth ministry. I, too, am in trial-and-error mode—trying everything possible and thinking outside the box as much as possible, as well as constantly reinforcing the truths in as many different ways as possible, that will change people's perspectives. Prayer is a big part at the start of intergenerational ministry.

—Mel, Youth Pastor in Australia

CLOSING THOUGHTS

As I mentioned in the Introduction, this book isn't offering a new model for ministry but a new mindset. My hope is that the various themes discussed in this book will open opportunities for further discussion with key leadership in your church or ministry. Hopefully, you have discovered some insights that you can apply in your ministry context. With this in mind, let me offer a few additional ideas to get those conversations started.

I love the idea of putting multiple generations together when we are talking about our teenagers. I wish that more "grandparents" in the church adopted these young people and were not frightened of them.

—Sandy, Parent of a Teenager

---

1. As you think about a ministry that's "customized" to the unique needs of each adolescent, let Jesus be your model. As he encountered people throughout his ministry, Jesus always tailored his message and teaching to the person he was hanging out with. Think of his encounter with Nicodemus, with the Samaritan woman at the well, or his interactions with his disciples. This means doing less large-group programming and more individual discipleship. Don't do away with all large-group settings (we need that space), but be sure to spend time equipping adults (especially your volunteers) to focus on each student in the local church. Use the objectives found in Appendix D as a starting point. This is not smaller thinking but specific and intentional thinking that will create bigger and deeper results in the long run.

2. Think holistically about helping adolescents mature and develop. It is imperative that we look at the whole student, not just the part of life that we think of as "spiritual." Think back on the list of Developmental Assets presented in chapter 2. With these internal and external assets at our fingertips, we need to network with other caring adults like principals, coaches, teachers, parents, and adult acquaintances who can provide a surrounding of full care. I recently received a letter from the school principals on my side of Denver who were seeking to partner with churches to create a caring community where students are loved and cared for. We need to look outside the walls of our church buildings and seek partnerships

with adults in secular settings who can partner with us to surround students with care and love. Go looking for these partnerships.

3. Work to establish a group of adults surrounding every student. One-on-one discipleship is needed, but each student needs a network of adults if he or she is to traverse through adolescence on their way to adult faith in Jesus Christ. Youth workers used to shoot for a ratio of one adult for every five students in a small-group environment. Today, I join with others in thinking that ratio needs to be flipped. We need five adults committed to every single adolescent. We need to surround young people with adults who love and support them. This different day requires an increased amount of support and love from the church family in all spaces.

   In the past, our church took one "baby step" toward providing such support for every youth through a prayer campaign we called "5 to 1 by 5/1." Our senior pastor and church leadership challenged the congregation to ensure that five adults were praying for each individual student in our care by May 1. This is a new idea around intergenerational ministry, but it is picking up steam as we head into the future.

4. We youth workers need to find ways to move from the center of the youth ministry to the outer circles. Too many current youth ministries revolve around the youth pastor. Students need to become the center of attention, surrounded by a "cloud of witnesses" offering love, support, sound teaching, and discipleship. We youth workers need to move away from thinking of ourselves primarily as "camp counselors" with responsibility over a small group of students. Instead we must see our primary goal as equipping the saints for ministry—especially parents. We become the facilitators (or networkers) who connect more adults with adolescents.

5. Parents need practical tools and resources. Many parents have very little idea what kind of developmental changes their adolescents are experiencing, other than the physical changes. They think the outside is a good indication of the inside—which isn't always the case. Youth workers have an opportunity to provide good information and pastoral support to help parents flourish as the primary spiritual caregivers. If anyone should be a faithful resource to parents, it should be those in the church who best understand the developmental and cultural issues surrounding youth today.

   At our church our children's, youth, and college ministries are partnering together to train and resource parents. Once a month we provide a "seminar" where parents come together to have dinner, hear a speaker who addresses a parenting or youth-related issue, and then break into discussion groups based on the ages of their children. This is a positive activity that offers useful training and helps parents connect with one another. By working together our three ministries to children and youth model partnership, while putting the emphasis of discipleship back in the hands of parents.

The best way to get most youth more involved in and serious about their faith communities is to get their *parents* more involved in and serious about their faith communities. For decades in many religious traditions, the prevailing model of youth ministry has relied on pulling teens away from their parents. In some cases, youth ministers have come to see parents as adversaries. There is no doubt a time and place for unique teen settings and activities; still, our findings suggest that overall youth ministry would probably best be pursued in a larger context of family ministry, that parents should be viewed as indispensable partners in the religious formation of youth.

—Christian Smith, *Soul Searching*

---

6. The whole church must wake up to the reality that the youth of today are the leaders of tomorrow's church. Unless we have a clear strategy for saving and equipping the adolescents in our care to become mature leaders (and saving those at the mall), many congregations will die due to inadequate leadership. Leadership development must start at younger ages with the involvement of the entire church. We must grab hold of the biblical idea of older generations pouring their spiritual lives into younger generations. The future of the church depends on it.

7. Finally, the goal of youth ministry must change. We must make a priority of assimilating adolescents fully into the family of God while they are still in junior and senior high. Helping teenagers become mature followers of Christ who are connected to a local intergenerational body of Christ dramatically increases the odds that they will remain connected to a local church after high school. Simply being plugged in to a youth group that meets weekly does not provide the same security. Our teenagers need to experience prophetic preaching from church leaders, baptism and the Lord's Supper with multiple generations, worship styles that make space for everyone, a strategic discipleship plan for the next generation that involves the whole church, and an organic body of believers who are serving and using their gifts in ministry. The next generation must become the lungs that join God's Spirit in breathing new life into the church.

I encourage you to take the themes in this book, pray for the Lord's guidance, dialogue with others, and experiment with some changes in your current programming. But most of all, I encourage you and your congregation or ministry to develop a new mindset that places priority on helping older generations invest sacrificially into younger generations. Go beyond gathering some volunteers to sit in the back of the room during youth meetings, and seek ways to intentionally and strategically connect parents and other adults with your youth. Be creative—finding ways to partner with caring adults both within the walls of the church and with the surrounding community.

Don't be afraid to take chances. You won't meet success with every attempt—but don't let this discourage you. Keep trying. Think about the game of baseball. They say hitting a baseball is one of the most difficult feats in all of sports (and my own childhood experience confirms this!). In the major leagues, a .300 batting average is the standard mark of an excellent hitter. Yet a player who hits .300 fails seven out of every ten times. I can't think of any other sport where a 30 percent success rate is considered a great success. But this makes having a positive mindset even more important.

The same is true as you seek to bring the ideas and perspective in this book into your everyday ministry. Will you be able to line up all the lenses every day? Probably not. Will you hit a home run with every swing? It's doubtful. The urgency of ministry and the demands of the day will take over unless you keep this new mindset at the forefront of your thinking. Keep swinging. Refer back to the themes in this book often. Use the retreat planning guide, Evaluation Tool, and other resources in the appendixes to help guide your approach. You might succeed only 30 percent of the time, but with God on your side, you will develop a ministry mindset that faithfully focuses on bringing adults and teenagers together for the transformation of the church.

I am in trial-and-error mode. I don't have success stories yet, just a general direction in which I am going. The emphasis for our 'Intergenerational Ministry' will be about coming alongside parents to equip and encourage them in the great calling of raising children in the Lord. Programmatically, I want the church to do what it can to help parents become the parents that God is calling and empowering them to be.

—Didi, Youth Pastor

LEARNING TO DANCE TOGETHER

I still remember dancing with my grandmother at the wedding of one of my older sisters. We still have a picture that was taken of us. In the photo I look embarrassed. I remember that I really did not know what I was doing at the time; it felt like we were just spinning in circles. But looking back on that one short life experience, I think it was beautiful. One generation leading another around the dance floor.

This is the future landscape of the church (and youth ministry within her) on beautiful display. When we begin to get our dance groove going on, we dance with a lot of different partners. We dance with parents. We dance with church elders and other lay leaders. We dance with families. We dance with teachers, school administrators, and athletic coaches. We dance with the senior pastor, other church staff, and our volunteer ministry leaders. We dance with a wide variety of other caring and Christ-following adults. And we encourage this whole community of leaders to reach out to our youth and invite them to share the floor with us. It becomes a beautiful image of God's reign here on earth as we minister to and with the next generation.

As we wrap up this conversation about a new mindset for reaching and discipling the next generation, I want to thank you for hanging in there with me. If you have made it this far, you deserve a huge hug or pat on the back. Thank you. But the real challenge still lies ahead.

Whether you are a youth worker, parent, senior pastor, elder, volunteer, or anyone else who has taken the time to think through these important themes, the time to act is now. We do not have the luxury of sitting back and waiting. Before we know it, the students in our care will grow up and become the leaders of the future local church. May we be faithful to help them grow in maturity and connect to an intergenerational body of believers. God bless you and your partners in ministry as you take risks to do ministry together.

Now to him who is able to do immeasurably more than all we ask or imagine, according to his power that is at work within us, to him be glory in the church and in Christ Jesus throughout all generations, for ever and ever! Amen.

—Paul in Ephesians 3:20–21

CONTINUE THE CONVERSATION

1. Which of the topics in this book require the most attention in rethinking your approach to ministry? Which lenses are already in focus?
2. How could you create more connecting and partnering with adolescents and older adults in the local church?
3. How can keeping in mind the different "spaces" strengthen your ministry?
4. What is the goal of your youth ministry? Does it involve connecting adolescents to the local church today? If not, how would adopting this goal change your weekly and monthly planning?
5. Which of the suggestions in this book will you seek to implement in the next month or year? What will you do to encourage an intergenerational approach throughout your ministry?

APPENDIX A
TOGETHER EVALUATION TOOL

ASSESSING THE MINDSET OF YOUR MINISTRY

These evaluation questions will allow you to consider how effective your current ministry is in addressing some of the themes and issues found in this book. You may find it helpful to contemplate these questions on your own, with your church leadership team, with parents, and with your team of volunteers and other caring adults. The scale allows you to assess your ministry's faithfulness or effectiveness in each area: 4—"doing very well," 3—"doing well," 2—"needs improvement," or 1—"not happening at all." Notice that there is no middle number, which helps the evaluator or group have to lean one way or another. I recognize this is a very linear approach to evaluating an organic animal of ministry, but it will help spur more conversation and dialogue around faithful intergenerational ministry. Consider using this tool in training meetings or on a leadership retreat.

THEOLOGY AND DISCIPLESHIP:

1. | **4 3 2 1** | Youth leaders have adequate formal theological training (Bible college, seminary, or other).

2. | **4 3 2 1** | Ministry programming is based on and tested by biblical truth and led by the Holy Spirit.

3. | **4 3 2 1** | Youth workers are committed to ongoing Bible study.

4. | **4 3 2 1** | Youth workers are sensitive to the Holy Spirit's counsel and are accountable to others.

5. | **4 3 2 1** | Youth workers are able to articulate biblical direction and vision based on an intergenerational mindset.

6. | **4 3 2 1** | Youth workers evaluate overall youth ministry programming through the lens of Trinitarian theology.

7. | **4 3 2 1** | Teaching is biblically faithful, sensitive to the Spirit, and fully connected to the whole of the church family.

ASSIMILATION AND COMMUNITY:

1. | **4 3 2 1** | The intentional vision of the youth ministry is to help young people connect to the intergenerational church body.

2. | **4 3 2 1** | Youth feel connected to the overall church body by the time they "graduate" from the youth program.

3. | **4 3 2 1** | Youth are connected in meaningful relationships with adults outside of their own families.

4. | **4 3 2 1** | Youth are active participants in the current life of the larger church, not just the youth group.

5. | **4 3 2 1** | Youth embrace and can articulate the congregation's mission, beliefs, and history.

6. | **4 3 2 1** | Youth workers are intentionally training and coaching parents to minister to their adolescent child(ren).

7. | **4 3 2 1** | Youth seek out ways to use their gifts and talents in service to others.

8. | **4 3 2 1** | Youth demonstrate a willingness to allow Jesus' teachings to impact their ethical and moral decision making.

9. | **4 3 2 1** | Youth demonstrate a commitment to personal spiritual disciplines like Bible study, prayer, fasting, solitude, and silence.

10. | **4 3 2 1** | Youth allow their discipleship journey to be influenced and supported by adult disciples.

11. | **4 3 2 1** | Youth show developmentally appropriate care and concern for the spiritual lives of others.

12. | **4 3 2 1** | All youth workers, volunteers, parents, and other adults are

being equipped with the theological, psychosocial, and cultural knowledge to disciple youth.

ADOLESCENCE AND FAMILIES:

1. | **4 3 2 1** | Youth workers understand that adolescents are neither "big children" nor "little adults," but experiencing a specific developmental phase of life.

2. | **4 3 2 1** | Youth workers know adolescents are trying to find themselves (Identity) whether those youth know it or not.

3. | **4 3 2 1** | Youth workers understand that adolescents are trying to figure out how they can operate on their own terms (Autonomy) whether those youth know it or not.

4. | **4 3 2 1** | Youth workers realize adolescents are trying to figure out how they connect to the larger picture or story of life (Belonging) whether those youth know it or not.

5. | **4 3 2 1** | Youth workers believe students live in "layers" or "selves," meaning they act differently depending on the group or situation they are in.

6. | **4 3 2 1** | Youth workers believe parents have the greatest spiritual influence in an adolescent's life.

7. | **4 3 2 1** | Youth workers plan programs evaluating family calendars and finances with an intergenerational mindset.

8. | **4 3 2 1** | Youth workers believe every student has a strong influencing peer group or cluster of friends.

CULTURE AND ENVIRONMENT:

1. | **4 3 2 1** | Youth workers take seriously and address the needs and concerns unique to adolescents and their development.

2. | **4 3 2 1** | Youth workers assess popular culture theologically and biblically.

3. | **4 3 2 1** | Youth ministry programming demonstrates sensitivity to the cultural context in which the church belongs (i.e., geography, tradition, leadership structure), but it is intergenerational in thinking.

4. | **4 3 2 1** | Youth ministry programming demonstrates sensitivity to global cultural issues (i.e., modern and postmodern thinking).

5. | **4 3 2 1** | The language used by youth ministry programs is easily understood within the culture of the larger congregation, as well as the broader culture.

6. | **4 3 2 1** | Our ministry provides an environment that is safe and accepting.

7. | **4 3 2 1** | Adolescents in our ministry are supported as they explore the hard questions of life and faith.

8. | **4 3 2 1** | The ministry provides opportunities for adults to invest in the lives of adolescents.

9. | **4 3 2 1** | Youth ministry teaching and programming is culturally relevant but biblically uncompromising.

THINKING TOGETHER ABOUT INTERGENERATIONAL MINISTRY

OUTLINE FOR A LEADERS RETREAT BASED ON THIS BOOK

I hope you finished reading this book full of enthusiasm—and also full of questions. Spend some time pondering the themes in this book. Make time to discuss them with the leadership of your church or ministry, the parents of the teenagers you work with, and other adult leaders and volunteers in ministry. You might consider using various chapters of this book as jumping-off places for ministry discussion at your regular leadership meetings, or you might build a full-day or overnight retreat to discuss an intergenerational approach to ministry with parents, volunteers, and other caring adults. It might be difficult to cover everything in this book in a single day, but a one-day event might be easier for your leaders to attend.

The following outline suggests a schedule for a daylong retreat discussing the material in this book. Hand out the book to your volunteer leaders and encourage them to read it prior to the retreat. Don't make the retreat itself a presentation of the book, but a discussion about implementing this new mindset in your ministry. The schedule can easily be adapted for a two-day overnight retreat with more breaks and additional relationship-building time. If your schedule permits, you may want to set aside time early in the retreat for participants to fill out and discuss the *"Together* Evaluation Tool" (Appendix A)—or ask people to fill out the assessment prior to the retreat. If you stick with a single day, the facilitator will need to keep the group on task. You may even want to appoint a timekeeper (carry a large clock with you!). Don't forget the snacks!

"TOGETHER" DAY RETREAT:

8:30–9:30 a.m.—Introduce "Doing Ministry Together."

- Use the book's Introduction as a reference for beginning the conversation about intergenerational ministry: "Intergener . . . What? Moving Toward a New Mind-set for Youth Ministry."
- Keep the "Mixed Mindset" and "Focused Mindset" pictures nearby for discussion.
- If you have the ability, do an Internet search on "intergenerational ministry" with the group.

9:30–10:30 a.m.—Discuss the shape of youth ministry today.

- Use Chapter 1: "What's Really Happening? The Youth Ministry State of Affairs."
- Use end-of-the-chapter questions to continue the conversation.

10:30–10:45 a.m.—Break

10:45 a.m.–12:00 p.m.—Discuss adolescent development.

- Use Chapter 2: "Getting Into Their Heads: Understanding Adolescent Development."
- Use end-of-the-chapter questions to continue the conversation.

12:00–1:00 p.m.—Lunch and discuss families and adolescents.

- Use Chapter 3: "Going Inside the Walls: Looking at Today's Family."
- Use end-of-the-chapter questions to continue the conversation.

1:00–1:15 p.m.—Break

1:15–2:00 p.m.—Discuss youth culture and its effect on youth ministry.

- Use Chapter 4: "Swimming Upstream: Riding the Waves of a Changing Culture."
- Use end-of-the-chapter questions to continue the conversation.

2:00–3:00 p.m.—Discuss what youth ministry leadership should look like.

- Use Chapter 5: "Being the Point Person: Thoughtful Reflections on Leadership."
- Use end-of-the-chapter questions to continue the conversation.

3:00–4:00 p.m.—Discuss the gospel message and the most effective methods for evangelism.

- Use Chapter 6: "Sharing the Good News: Embracing New Forms of Evangelism."
- Use end-of-the-chapter questions to continue the conversation.

4:00–4:15 p.m.—Break

4:15–5:00 p.m.—Discuss what discipleship should look like with adolescents.

- Use Chapter 7: "From Older to Younger: Reviving Discipleship to the Next Generation."
- Use end-of-the-chapter questions to continue the conversation.

5:00–6:00 p.m.—Dinner and Discuss "The Parable of the Yepherd."

- Before the meal begins, have someone read aloud "The Parable of the Yepherd."
- Use end-of-the-chapter questions to continue the conversation.

6:00–6:15 p.m.—Break

6:15–8:00 p.m.—Discuss what an "intergenerational ministry mindset" might look like in your ministry context.

- Use the Conclusion: "Transforming the Church Together: Gaining a New Mindset for Intergenerational Ministry."
- Use end-of-the-chapter questions to continue the conversation.
- You might consider doing a SWOT Analysis (Strengths, Weaknesses, Opportunities, and Threats) of your ministry in light of your new mindset. Be sure to record the results of your SWOT Analysis for later reference.

8:00 p.m.—Pray

A WORKING MINDSET FOR INTERGENERATIONAL MINISTRY

MISSION STRATEGIES FROM FOOTHILLS BIBLE CHURCH

Here is a working plan that illustrates how one congregation is seeking to bring teenagers and adults together in cross-generational ministry. During my time on the pastoral staff of Foothills Bible Church in Littleton, Colorado, I've been part of many conversations about adopting a more intentionally intergenerational mindset in our ministries with youth. This plan represents where we are today—but understand that it is a work in progress. Our ministry is continually changing and being adapted based on the principles in this book and the mission of our church. Adaptability and change are more keys to organic ministry that connects adolescents to the whole of the church.

THE MISSION OF FOOTHILLS BIBLE CHURCH

"A Family—Upward, Inward, and Outward"

"To glorify God (Ephesians 3:21) by growing as a spiritual family (1 Timothy 3:15) through evangelizing unbelievers (Acts 2:47) establishing all believers (Romans 1:11) in the Holy Scriptures (2 Timothy 3:16–17) by the Holy Spirit (Acts 1:8) in order that everyone in the FBC family will participate in worshipping our God (Romans 12:1), building up his church (Ephesians 4:11–16), and reaching out to our local (Colossians 4:5–6) and global community (Acts 13:1–3)."

FBC STUDENT MINISTRY MISSION (JR. HIGH, SR. HIGH, AND COLLEGE/CAREER)

"To help students on the journey to becoming mature Jesus-following adults who are connected to the church family."

PRIMARY STRATEGIES

Focus One: Empower Parents of Teenagers with Information and Training.

Offer Sunday morning four-to-six-week class for parents once a year (April/May), biannual parent meetings (September/January), monthly parent training for parents of students ages five through college-aged students; use Web page, newsletter, and monthly connections publication to provide information and resources for parents.

Focus Two: Equip the Extended Family of Foothills Bible Church.

Use monthly publication, leadership meeting, vision casting, collaboration, and communication with leadership team and ministry directors.

Focus Three: Filter All Through an Intergenerational Ministry Mindset.

Plan leadership meetings, student ministry staff meetings, volunteer meetings; Consider the church calendar, financial costs to families and the congregation, student ministry partnership with other ministries.

Focus Four: Create a Few Faithful Age-Specific Programming Environments

Sunday morning "Get Schooled" for junior and senior high, midweek programming, service/missions projects, outreach events, retreats, and fun activities.

STUDENT MINISTRY GOALS AND OBJECTIVES

1. Proactively help students find at least five caring Jesus-following adults to support and pray for them on the journey to becoming a mature Jesus-following adult (a constellation of supportive adults).

   - *Staff and volunteers build relationships with every student and his/her family.*
   - *Speak to each student to find out what caring adults he/she has already.*

- *Survey the entire group to find out what caring adults they have already.*
- *Create a database to track the five adults in each student's life.*
- *Have regular training meetings with all adults.*
- *Cast vision to the overall church body to surround every student.*
- *Regularly pray for caring adults to surround students.*

2. Purposely connect every student weekly to the larger FBC family in worship services and serving opportunities.

- *Invite every student to attend a main service on the weekend.*
- *Directors and volunteers are available to sit with students during services.*
- *Volunteers and staff model attendance in the main service on weekends.*
- *Invite students to serve in other areas of the church on Sunday morning.*
- *Partner with other ministries in teaching and service that connects with students.*
- *Continue conversations at the leadership level about service and partnerships.*
- *Regularly pray for students to get connected to the whole church body.*

3. Over a six-year period, share the gospel multiple times with every student, giving them all the chance to become followers of Jesus Christ.

- *Encourage student attendance at Sunday morning worship services where the gospel is shared.*
- *Strategically plan, as part of the curriculum, times when the gospel will be presented.*
- *Plan calendar events when the gospel will be presented.*
- *Brainstorm creative ways for students to respond to the gospel.*
- *Regularly pray for the salvation of students.*

4. Over a six-year period, teach every student the whole of Scripture using both Old and New Testaments.

- *Attend Sunday morning worship services.*
- *Plot out a six-year calendar so the whole of Scripture is presented to every student (this will be strategic in giving students broad strokes of the Bible).*

5. Over a six-year period, teach students spiritual practices to own their faith (i.e., personal Bible study, prayer, silence, solitude, worship, service, evangelism, and journaling).

- *Calendar when these spiritual practices will be taught over a six-year period.*
- *Brainstorm programming times and/or retreats where these spiritual practices will be taught and used.*

- *Creatively use one-on-one discipleship, small groups, and large-group environments to train students in spiritual practices.*

6. Develop effective weekly small- and large-group environments for students to experience God, fellowship with friends, and connect with spiritually mature Jesus-following adults.

   - *Sunday morning (8:45 hour on campus).*
     JH "Get Schooled Bible Study"—Directors/Volunteer Teachers.
     SH "Get Schooled Bible Study"—Directors/Volunteer Teachers.
   - *Sunday morning (10:45 hour in sanctuary)—All students in main services.*
   - *Sunday morning—Other intergenerational "Sunday school" options for teenagers to join adults.*
   - *Tuesday night (6:30–8:30 p.m. on campus)—JH large-group worship and teaching by directors and small-group sessions with volunteer leaders.*
   - *Wednesday night (6:30–8:30 p.m. on campus)—SH large-group worship and teaching by directors and small-group sessions with volunteer leaders.*
   - *Sunday night fun connecting points.*

7. Provide regular and consistent information and training to parents of teenagers.

   - *Provide regular four-to-six-week Sunday morning class series on "Parenting Teenagers" or a Saturday "Parenting Teenagers Training Seminar."*
   - *Provide electronic newsletter to parents with advice, resources, and ministry updates.*
   - *Change and update Web page with helpful information for parents.*
   - *Hold two meetings each year (in September and February) for parents of junior and senior high students (together or separate).*
   - *Hold monthly parent training opportunities in partnership with children's ministry.*

8. Provide a few purposeful regular on/off-campus environments that contribute to our student ministry, including service and missions.

   - *Summer mission opportunities with adults.*
   - *Service days with adults.*
   - *Outreach opportunities (periodically on Sunday nights) with adults.*
   - *Partner with other FBC ministries (i.e., Vacation Bible School, children's ministry, adults).*

9. Pray monthly for every student in our ministry (and his/her family).

   - *Collect database of youth and families to be given to each volunteer leader.*

- *Pray weekly for a few families in the student ministries at each regular staff meeting, so that all are prayed for over the course of each month.*

10. Hold weekly staff meetings with directors and administrative assistant and monthly meetings with JH and SH volunteer leaders.

- *Provide leadership training monthly to volunteer leaders.*
- *Evaluate how we are doing at accomplishing our mission.*
- *Build unity and teamwork around an intergenerational mindset.*

APPENDIX D
OBJECTIVES FOR DISCIPLESHIP
MARKERS ON THE PATHWAY TO MATURITY IN CHRIST

Many have tried to boil Christian discipleship down to a few steps, but we know intuitively that helping adolescents walk more closely to Jesus demands more than learning a couple of principles, taking a six-week class, or memorizing a few verses. We're talking about guiding people in establishing a daily lifestyle of living for the Triune God.

In thinking about the elements of discipleship, I've found a list that LeRoy Eims has developed to be very helpful in ministry to adolescents. I have changed and adapted his list of discipleship objectives a bit to fit our mindset for ministry.[1] Thousands have used these objectives as a way of defining discipleship in all different situations and ministry contexts. Think of it as a way of helping those you disciple develop skills and habits that reflect the whole of the gospel.

DISCIPLESHIP OBJECTIVES

1. **Assurance of Salvation**—Share your confidence in your salvation with one another (John 1:12–13; Romans 8:16; 1 John 5:11–13; Jude 1, 24).
2. **Specific Daily Time with God**—Have a daily time of prayer and Bible study (Genesis 19:27; Exodus 34:2-3; Psalm 5:3; Daniel 6:10; Mark 1:35; 1 Corinthians 1:9).
3. **Winning over Sin**—Resist sin consistently, so you grow in holiness (Isaiah 41:13; 1 Corinthians 10:13; 15:57).
4. **Separating Ourselves from Sin**—Avoid sin by taking specific steps (Romans 6:12–14; 12:1–2; 2 Corinthians 6:14–18; 2 Timothy 2:19–22; James 1:12; 1 John 1:5–2:2; 2:15–16).

177

5. **Time with Believers**—Be consistent in local church attendance and other fellowship opportunities with Christians (Psalm 122:1; Acts 2:42; Hebrews 10:24-25; 1 John 1:3).

6. **The Bible**—Learn to articulate your belief in the inspiration of Scripture (Psalm 19:7-11; 119:105, 160; Matthew 22:29; 2 Timothy 3:16-17; 2 Peter 1:21).

7. **Hearing the Bible**—Meditate on the Scriptures and apply their teachings to your life (Proverbs 28:9; Jeremiah 22:29; Luke 19:48).

8. **Reading the Bible**—Intentionally read through the whole Bible (Deuteronomy 17:19; 1 Timothy 4:13; Revelation 1:3).

9. **Bible Study**—Study specific sections of the Bible using various resources and tools (Ezra 7:10; Proverbs 2:1-5; Acts 17:11).

10. **Bible Memory**—Regularly memorize and internalize portions of Scripture for recall (Deuteronomy 6:6-7; Psalm 37:31; Proverbs 7:1-3; Matthew 4:4; Colossians 3:16).

11. **Meditation on the Bible**—Reflect on what you are learning about God and yourself because of Bible reading and study (Joshua 1:8; Psalm 1; Jeremiah 15:16; Philippians 4:8).

12. **Application of the Bible**—Apply the Bible to personal life circumstances (Psalm 119:56-60; Luke 6:46-49; 2 Timothy 3:16-17; James 1:22-25).

13. **Taking to God** (Prayer)—Pray daily on an ongoing basis (Matthew 6:6; 7:7; 21:22; John 17; Ephesians 6:18; Philippians 4:6-7; 1 Thessalonians 5:17; James 5:17; 1 John 3:22).

14. **Sharing your Story** (Testimony)—Learn to share how you came to trust Jesus as Savior (Luke 8:38-39; John 9:25; Acts 26:1-23; 1 John 1:3).

15. **Lordship of Christ**—Grow in allowing Jesus to control every area of your life (Luke 6:46; Romans 12:1-2; Colossians 1:18; Hebrews 1:2).

16. **Faith**—Trust God with specific needs (Romans 4:20-21; Ephesians 6:16; Hebrews 11:6; 1 John 5:4).

17. **Love**—Show love, concern, and compassion toward others in service (John 13:34-35; 1 Corinthians 13:4-7; 15:13; 1 John 3:17-18; 4:7-21).

18. **Speaking**—Demonstrate control over your tongue so encouragement is consistent (Psalm 71:15; Proverbs 18:6-7; 26:20; Ephesians 4:29; Colossians 4:6; James 1:26; 3:1-12).

19. **The Use of Time**—Develop the ability to manage time and schedule well (Psalm 90:10, 12; Proverbs 31:27; Ecclesiastes 3:1; Romans 13:11; Ephesians 5:15-17; James 4:14).

20. **The Will of God**—Seek and follow God's direction in one's life (Psalm 119:105; Proverbs 15:22; John 16:13; Romans 12:1-2).

21. **Obeying God**—Submit consistently to God's direction with a joyful heart (1 Samuel 15:22; Psalm 119:59–60; Job 17:9; John 14:21, 23; 15:10, 14; James 4:17).

22. **The Holy Spirit**—Experience the working of the Holy Spirit in one's life (Zechariah 4:6; John 14:16–17; 15:26–27; 16:7–8, 13–15; Romans 8:5–6, 16–17, 26; 12:3–8; 1 Corinthians 12:13–14; Galatians 5:22–23; Ephesians 5:18).

23. **Rejecting Satan** (our enemy)—Stand against the enemy and help others do the same (Isaiah 14:12–15; Matthew 4:4; John 8:44; 2 Corinthians 2:11; 4:3–4; 10:3–5; Ephesians 6:10–18; 1 Peter 5:8–9; 1 John 4:4).

24. **Dealing with Sin**—Be willing to share areas of sin with others for accountability and develop a plan of action to overcome sin (Mark 14:38; Romans 13:14; Ephesians 6:10–20; Colossians 3:9–10; 1 Peter 1:14–16; 1 John 1:9).

25. **Forgiveness**—Accept God's forgiveness and be willing to forgive others (Psalm 32:1; Matthew 5:23–24; 18:15; 1 John 1:9).

26. **Second Coming of Christ**—Be secure in your understanding that Jesus is returning to establish his kingdom (John 14:2–3; 1 Thessalonians 4:16–17; Titus 2:11–14; 1 John 3:2–3; Revelation 19:11–16).

27. **Sharing Our Faith**—Initiate sharing the good news with others (Proverbs 28:1; 11:30; John 4; Acts 8:35; Romans 1:16; 1 Corinthians 15:3–4; Colossians 1:28–29; 2 Timothy 4:1–2).

28. **Following Up to Sharing Faith**—Encourage those with whom you have shared the gospel (Colossians 1:28; 2 Timothy 1:3; 2:2; 3 John 4).

29. **Giving Financially**—Give money regularly to the Lord's work (Proverbs 3:9–10, 27; 11:24–25; Malachi 3:10; Luke 6:38; 2 Corinthians 8:9; 9:6–8; Galatians 6:6).

30. **Becoming a World Christian**—Show interest and concern for the whole world coming to know Jesus (Isaiah 6:8; Matthew 9:35–28; 28:18–20; Mark 16:15; Luke 24:47; John 20:21; Acts 1:8).

This list is not an exhaustive list of all that the "whole will of God" might include. But it is a good starting point for seeking to develop one's own discipleship fully and share it with others. This list provides markers along the path to maturity in Christ. It can also be used as goals or objectives for every student in your ministry. As we spend time investing in the lives of particular young people, we will get to know these students well and can customize a discipleship path for each of them. If an adolescent is struggling with a particular element on the list, the discipler can spend some time teaching on this topic. If love or faith is lacking, time reflecting and praying on these topics in discipleship meetings is the prescription.

Think of these thirty items not so much as a checklist or a step-by-step model for discipleship as a way of nurturing a mindset to guide our thinking as we disciple the next generation with faithfulness.

NOTES

INTRODUCTION

1. Article can be read here: http://www.youthworker.com/resources/ministry/11579044/ (accessed September 2009).
2. You may see all of their current research and articles at www.fulleryouthinstitute.com.

CHAPTER 1

1. Sam Rainer III and Thom S. Rainer discuss the importance of the next generation experiencing the local church as important to their lives in their book, *Essential Church?* (Nashville: B&H Publishing Group, 2008).
2. I have read national research ranging from 50 to 74 percent of students leave the church upon high school graduation. Some return after getting married or having children, but others never do. This is tragic!
3. Doug Fields, *Your First Two Years in Youth Ministry* (Grand Rapids, MI: Youth Specialties/Zondervan 2002), 37–38.
4. David Elkind, *All Grown Up and No Place to Go* (Cambridge, MA: Perseus Books, 1998), 3.
5. Kenda Creasy Dean and Ron Foster, *The Godbearing Life: The Art of Soul Tending for Youth Ministry* (Nashville: Upper Room Books, 1998), 212.
6. Jeff Baxter, *Following Jesus into College and Beyond* (Grand Rapids, MI: Youth Specialties/Zondervan, 2009).
7. Chap Clark addresses this topic of living in the underground world in his book *Hurt: Inside the World of Today's Teenagers* (Grand Rapids, MI: Baker Books, 2004). We will address this topic further in the next chapter.
8. Merton Strommen and Richard Hardel, *Passing on the Faith* (Winona, MN: Saint Mary's Press), 66–67.
9. Based on research from the book by Steve Farkas and Jean Johnson, *Kids These Days: What Americans Really Think About the Next Generation* (New York: Public Agenda, 1997), 8–9.

CHAPTER 2

1. Mentor Foundation, "Teenage Brain Development and Vulnerability to Drug Use," www.mentorfoundation.org/brain (accessed November 2009).

2. "Inside the Teenage Brain," a PBS special *Frontline* interview with Dr. Geidd about his research, along with other professionals in the field of adolescent brain research. You can read more at www.pbs.org/wgbh/pages/frontline/shows/teenbrain/interviews/giedd.html (accessed November 2009).

3. From Slide Share presentation by Dr. Ken Winters, professor in Dept. of Psychiatry at University of Minnesota, www.mentorfoundation.org/brain (accessed November 2009).

4. "Inside the Teenage Brain," a PBS special *Frontline* interview with Dr. Deborah Yurgelun-Todd, director of neuropsychology and cognitive neuroimaging at McLean Hospital in Belmont, Massachusetts. You can read more at www.pbs.org/wgbh/pages/frontline/shows/teenbrain/interviews/todd.html (accessed November 2009).

5. Doug Gross, "Social Networks and Kids: How young is too young." CNN.com (accessed December 8, 2009).

6. Dr. Chap Clark and researchers at Fuller Theological Seminary have used the phrase "systematic abandonment" to describe what is currently happening around adolescents.

7. Louise J. Kaplan, *Adolescence: The Farewell to Childhood* (New York: Touchstone, 1984), 281.

8. Kaplan, 51.

9. In *Do Hard Things* (Multnomah, 2008), the Harris brothers argue that raising the bar and creating higher expectations for teenagers will take them out of their "shackles of the idea of adolescence and teenager" (pg. 34). I respectfully disagree with their loose definitions of these words.

10. The premise of *Do Hard Things* (Multnomah, 2008) is very good overall, but it misses sound research in the area of adolescence. Of course there are many teenagers doing wonderful things for the glory of God; but overall, there is still a developmental hurdle to get over where abandonment exists.

11. Chap Clark, "The Changing Face of Adolescence: A Theological View of Human Development," in *Starting Right* (Grand Rapids, MI: Youth Specialties/Zondervan, 2001), 45.

12. Both the American Medical Association and the United States Centers for Disease Control point to these age changes over the years. Their webpages are www.ama-assn.org and www.cdc.gov.

13. Jeff Baxter, *Following Jesus into College and Beyond* (Grand Rapids, MI: Youth Specialties/Zondervan, 2009), 16.

14. Clark, *"The Changing Face of Adolescence,"* 52.

15. Researchers and writers such as Dr. David Elkind, Dr. Carl G. Jung, Dr. Chap Clark, Dr. Kara Eckmann Powell, and many others are the most influential in these areas. Fuller Theological Seminary has developed specific research in this area. Their Web site is www.fulleryouthinstitute.org.

16. Carl G. Jung, *Personality Types* (Princeton: Princeton University Press, 1971), 448.

17. Chris O'Brien, "My Journey into the Heart of Generation Y Shopping Habits" (accessed from *The Mercury News* on December 8, 2009 from www.bbs.fltrp.com/archiver/?tid–35384.htm/).

18. For more about what's happening with adolescents, I recommend Chap Clark's book *Hurt: Inside the World of Today's Teenagers* (Grand Rapids, MI: Baker Books, 2004).

19. Mark DeVries, *Family-Based Youth Ministry* (Downer's Grove, IL: InterVarsity, 1994), 39.

20. This was a study done by the U.S. Council of Economic Advisors on Teenagers. Solarz, American Psychological Association, (May 2000), 4.

21. O'Brien, "My Journey into the Heart of Generation Y Shopping Habits."

22. The Search Institute (www.search-institute.org) was founded in 1958 to research the decline of children and teenage development as it related to the church, school, and community. After extensive research for several decades, Search Institute has put a mark in well-documented research that church involvement and religious faith has a significant impact on adolescents' positive development.

23. Peter L. Benson, *All Kids Are Our Kids* (San Francisco: Jossey-Bass Publishers, 1997), 4.

24. For more details on these assets and a copy to download for ministry purposes, go to www.search-institute.org.

25. Merton P. Strommen and Richard A. Hardel, in their book *Passing on the Faith* do a good job of explaining Peter Benson's list of Developmental Assets.

26. Research from Sam Rainer III and Thom S. Rainer's book *Essential Church?* (Nashville, TN: B&H Publishing Group, 2008) shows that when teens see "hypocrisy" in adults and parents, it has a lasting effect on the spiritual development of those adolescents.

CHAPTER 3

1. AP/MTV poll, OR Associated Press, August 20, 2007.

2. Jeffrey J. Arnett, "Adolescent Storm and Stress, Reconsidered," *Readings on Adolescence and Emerging Adulthood,* ed. Jeffrey J. Arnett (Upper Saddle River, NJ: Prentice Hall, 2002), 10.

3. Horatio Alger Association, *The State of Our Nation's Youth,* Washington, D.C. 2005–2006, 32.

4. George Barna, *Third Millennium Teens: Research on the Minds, Hearts and Souls of America's Teenagers* (Barna Research Group, 1999).

5. George Barna, *Third Millennium Teens.*

6. *Weekly Reader* Research, American Bible Society survey, February 5, 2007.

7. The Center for Youth and Family Ministry, October 2006.

8. Accessed from www.YPulse.com, November 2009.

9. National Campaign to Prevent Teen and Unplanned Pregnancy survey, January 2009.

10. Ibid.

11. From IG's Trend Central's Tween Intelligence Report (created for marketers), 65 percent of "tweens" (ages 10–12) look to a parent as a role model.

12. Barbara Kantrowitz and Karen Springen in *Newsweek,* April 25, 2005.

13. Jess Weiner, Global Ambassador for the Dove Self-Esteem Fund (*Real Girls, Real Pressure: A National Report on the State of Self-Esteem,* Dove Self-Esteem Fund study, October 8, 2008).

14. Accessed from www.mayoclinic.org (November 2009).

15. Study from "Teens Today," September 6, 2008.

16. Opinion Research Corporation, *Peoria Journal Star,* September 6, 2008.

17. Teens Research Unlimited, *USA Today,* April 14, 2008.

18. Harris Interactive, Trends & Tudes, October 2005.

19. Barna Research Group, www.barna.org, October 23, 2000.

20. The Center for Youth and Family Ministry, Fuller Theological Seminary, October 2006.

21. Rick Lawrence, *Jesus-Centered Youth Ministry* (Loveland, CO: Group Publishing, 2007), 146.

22. Judy Woodruff, "Generation Next Project," www.YPulse.com, January 2, 2007.

23. "The Millennial Values" online research study, The N press release, April 30, 2007.

24. Barna Research, "Research Shows that Spiritual Maturity Process Should Start at a Young Age," November 17, 2003.

25. Barna Research, "Parents Accept Responsibility for Their Child's Spiritual Development But Struggle with Effectiveness," May 6, 2003.

26. Ibid.

27. Ibid.

28. Reggie Joiner, *Think Orange* (Colorado Springs, CO: David C. Cook Publishers, 2009), 164.

29. Strommen and Hardel, *Passing on the Faith,* 66–67.

CHAPTER 4

1. Robert N. Bellah, et al., *Habits of the Heart* (Berkeley, CA: University of California Press, 1985).
2. Bellah, *Habits,* 82.
3. Leonard Sweet, *SoulTsunami* (Grand Rapids, MI: Zondervan, 1999), 84.
4. Accessed December 2009 from www.didyouknow.org in the technology section.
5. George Barna, *Real Teens: A Contemporary Snapshot of Youth Culture* (Ventura, CA: Regal Books, 2001), 35.
6. Facts on technology were accessed December 2009 from www.didyouknow.org.
7. David Elkind, *The Hurried Child* (Cambridge, MA: Perseus Books, 2001), 29.
8. Marshall McLuhan, *Understanding Media* (New York: Mentor, 1964).
9. H. Richard Niebuhr, *Christ and Culture* (New York: Harper and Row, 1951), 83.
10. Niebuhr, 127.
11. Duffy Robbins, *This Way to Youth Ministry* (Grand Rapids, MI: Youth Specialties/Zondervan, 2004), 256.

CHAPTER 5

1. Mike Bonem and Roger Patterson, *Leading from the Second Chair* (San Francisco: Jossey-Bass, 2005).
2. A. W. Tozer quote. Accessed January 2009 from http://www.crossroad.to/Excerpts/books/faith/Tozer/tozer-quotes.htm.
3. John Maxwell, *Developing the Leader Within You* (Nashville: Thomas Nelson, 1993).
4. Hans Finzel, *The Top Ten Mistakes Leaders Make* (Colorado Springs: Chariot Victor Publishing, 1994), 16.
5. George Bernard Shaw, *Man and Superman* (London: Penguin Group, 1972), 84.
6. Doug Fields, *Your First Two Years in Youth Ministry*, 173–178.
7. Many youth ministry professionals have written about the importance of surrounding youth with adults, but Mark DeVries uses the phrase "constellation of adults" in his book *Sustainable Youth Ministry* (Colorado Springs: InterVarsity Press, 2008).
8. Peter Scazzero, *The Emotionally Healthy Church: A Strategy for Discipleship That Actually Changes Lives* (Grand Rapids, MI: Zondervan, 2003), 103.

CHAPTER 6

1. Vaclav Havel, "The Need for Transcendence in the Postmodern World," *The Futurist* 29 (1995), 47.

2. Chuck Swindoll, *Hope for Our Troubled Times* (Plano, TX: Insight for Living, 2009), 10–11.

3. Francis A. Schaeffer, *The Great Evangelical Disaster* (Westchester, IL: Crossway Books, 1984), 37.

4. This phrase came out of discussions in the classroom at Fuller Theological Seminary among theologians, professors, and students.

5. Francis Chan, *Forgotten God: Reversing Our Tragic Neglect of the Holy Spirit* (Colorado Springs: David C. Cook, 2009), 36.

6. N. T. Wright, *Following Jesus: Biblical Reflections on Discipleship* (Grand Rapids, MI: Eerdmans, 1994), ix.

7. As I've considered the best starting point and method for sharing the gospel with the next generation, my thinking has been shaped by the ideas of James Choung in this article in *Christianity Today*: http://www.christianitytoday.com/ct/2008/july/11.31.html.

8. My wife, Laurie Baxter, developed this summary of the whole of Scripture and illustrated it on poster board for a class at Columbia International University with Dr. Mary Faith Philips.

9. Keith Drury and David Drury, *Ageless Faith: A Conversation between Generations about Church* (Indianapolis: Wesleyan Publishing House, 2010), 37–38.

CHAPTER 7

1. See www.sacredoutfitter.blogspot.com.

2. Of course, the book of Acts provides a model and a plan for multiplying churches, not just individuals.

3. This section was inspired by LeRoy Eims' faithful book on discipleship called *The Lost Art of Disciple Making* (Zondervan, 1978).

4. Dallas Willard, "The Spirit Is Willing: The Body as a Tool for Spiritual Growth" in *The Christian Educator's Handbook on Spiritual Formation*, ed. Kenneth O. Gangel and James C. Wilhoit (Wheaton, IL: Victor Books, 1994), 225.

5. Francis Cosgrove, *Essentials of Discipleship* (Colorado Springs: NavPress, 1980).

6. Duffy Robbins, *This Way to Youth Ministry*, 384.

7. Nick Taylor, "Spiritual Formation: Nurturing Spiritual Vitality" in *Introducing Christian Education: Foundations for the Twenty-First Century*, ed. Michael Anthony (Grand Rapids, MI: Baker, 2001), 91.

8. Alister McGrath, *The Journey: A Pilgrim in the Lands of the Spirit* (New York: Doubleday, 1999), 9.

CONCLUSION

1. Research taken from Carol S. Dweck, *Mindset* (New York: Random House, 2006), and from Michael Graham Richard's blog about Dweck's work (accessed October 16, 2009), http://michaelgr.com/2007/04/15/fixed-mindset-vs-growth-mindset-which-one-are-you/.
2. Kara Powell, "Is the Era of Age Segregation Over?" *Leadership Journal,* (Summer 2009), 43–47.
3. Joseph Myers, *In Search of Belonging* (Grand Rapids, MI: Zondervan, 2003).
4. Natalie Ferjulian and Maggie Roth, "Addicted to Facebook? Social Media and Christian Students," *YouthWorker Journal* (January/February 2010), 29.
5. Cited in Randy Frazee, *The Connecting Church: Beyond Small Groups to Authentic Community* (Grand Rapids, MI: Zondervan, 2001), 85.
6. For a great discussion on the importance of us not abandoning organized local churches with buildings, elders, and regular assemblies, read Kevin DeYoung and Ted Kluck's book *Why We Love the Church: In Praise of Institutions and Organized Religion* (Chicago: Moody Publishers, 2009).
7. Dietrich Bonhoeffer, *The Cost of Discipleship* (New York: Macmillan, 1959), 281.

APPENDIX D

1. LeRoy Eims, *The Lost Art of Disciple Making* (Grand Rapids, MI: Zondervan, 1978), 75.

Share Your Thoughts

With the Author: Your comments will be forwarded to the author when you send them to *zauthor@zondervan.com*.

With Zondervan: Submit your review of this book by writing to *zreview@zondervan.com*.

Free Online Resources at
www.zondervan.com

Zondervan AuthorTracker: Be notified whenever your favorite authors publish new books, go on tour, or post an update about what's happening in their lives at www.zondervan.com/authortracker.

Daily Bible Verses and Devotions: Enrich your life with daily Bible verses or devotions that help you start every morning focused on God. Visit www.zondervan.com/newsletters.

Free Email Publications: Sign up for newsletters on Christian living, academic resources, church ministry, fiction, children's resources, and more. Visit www.zondervan.com/newsletters.

Zondervan Bible Search: Find and compare Bible passages in a variety of translations at www.zondervanbiblesearch.com.

Other Benefits: Register yourself to receive online benefits like coupons and special offers, or to participate in research.

ZONDERVAN®

ZONDERVAN.com/
AUTHORTRACKER
follow your favorite authors